WITHDRAWN

D1287473

INTERNATIONAL STUDIES

of the
Committee on International Relations
University of Notre Dame

INTERNATIONAL STUDIES
of the
Committee on International Relations
University of Notre Dame

Why Democracies Fail
A Critical Evaluation of the Causes for
Modern Dictatorship
NORMAN L. STAMPS

Christian Democracy in Western Europe, 1820–1953
MICHAEL P. FOGARTY

The Fate of East Central Europe: Hopes and
Failures of American Foreign Policy
Edited by STEPHEN D. KERTESZ

German Protestants Face the Social Question
WILLIAM O. SHANAHAN

Diplomacy in a Whirlpool:
Hungary Between Nazi Germany and Soviet Russia
STEPHEN D. KERTESZ

Soviet Imperialism: Its Origins and Tactics
Edited by WALDEMAR GURIAN

Pan-Slavism: Its History and Ideology
HANS KOHN

The Foreign Policy of the British Labour Government
M. A. FITZSIMONS

Christian Democracy in Italy and France
MARIO EINAUDI *and* FRANCOIS GOGUEL

Bolshevism: An Introduction to Soviet Communism
WALDEMAR GURIAN

Europe Between Democracy and Anarchy
FERDINAND A. HERMENS

Out of Print

The Soviet Union: Background, Ideology, Reality
Edited by WALDEMAR GURIAN

The Catholic Church in World Affairs
Edited by WALDEMAR GURIAN *and*
M. A. FITZSIMONS

WHY DEMOCRACIES FAIL

A Critical Evaluation of the

Causes for Modern Dictatorship

WHY DEMOCRACIES FAIL

A Critical Evaluation of the

Causes for Modern Dictatorship

NORMAN L. STAMPS

UNIVERSITY OF NOTRE DAME PRESS

1957

JC
421
S 69

Library of Congress Catalog Card Number 57-9234
© 1957, University of Notre Dame Press
Notre Dame, Indiana

To My Parents and My Wife

For Their Confidence and Encouragement

PREFACE

T HIS little book is not intended to be an exhaustive treatise. It is instead a modest attempt to determine the major reasons for the collapse of parliamentary institutions and the rise of dictatorships. During the last few years a number of important studies have been made by political scientists, sociologists, economists, and psychologists; and there is already a great deal of literature in the field. However, most writers have been interested in an individual country, in a particular thesis, or in developing a single explanation; and few authors have attempted to survey the work that has been done, analyze it, and bring together in a single book the results obtained thus far.

The purpose of this study, therefore, is to discuss the major explanations offered by others for the failure of democracy and the rise of dictatorship. The author has not attempted to develop a new theory or an over-all explanation but to determine wherein and to what extent the existing theories are useful and provide a valid explanation. Little attention has been given to the use of terror, to the techniques used by dictatorships after they are in power, or to their organization, philosophies, or programs. Emphasis is placed primarily on why it was that popular government has been repudiated in so many European countries and why representative institutions were no longer felt to fill a need. A study of this kind is valuable because a better knowledge of the reasons for the decline and disintegration of parliamentary institutions should lead to a better understanding of the nature of democracy and the conditions under which it may be preserved.

It is, of course, possible to expand this little book in a number of directions. Most of the subjects touched upon are capable of and indeed in themselves demand a more extensive discussion. However, the object was to acquaint the general reader with the broad trends and the general changes that are taking place, the difficulties confronting democracies at the present time, and the reasons for the rise of dictatorship. Wherever possible an effort has been made to avoid the repetition of information readily available in the standard textbooks, and those who desire a more detailed discussion of institutional arrangements are advised to consult one of the leading texts in the field.

Some will be disappointed because there is no discussion of the intellectual basis of fascism and little on the theoretical background of communism. Vilfredo Pareto, Robert Michels, Oswald Spengler, Carl Schmitt, and Alfred Rosenberg have made their contributions. One could expand the circle a little further to include Gaetano Mosca, Georges Sorel, and Friedrich Nietzsche. One train of thought beginning with Hegel leads through Marx to communism; another beginning also with Hegel leads to fascism and nazism. Such a study could also be supplemented by quotations from Benito Mussolini's *Doctrine of Fascism* and Adolf Hitler's *Mein Kampf* as well as from the writings of Lenin and Stalin. There is no doubt that the whole idea of the state in Italy and Germany is different from that held in Great Britain and the United States. However, if the author must offer an excuse for this omission, it is that the inclusion of this material would make the book too large, that fascism is essentially anti-intellectual, that excellent studies tracing the evolution of fascist theory are already available, and that neither Italian Fascism nor German National Socialism ever developed a well-rounded philosophical system. The theoretical basis of communism is already well known, and under these circumstances it seemed wiser to limit this study to questions which attract a wider audience and have a greater interest.

Since the variability of terminology is one of the difficulties of political science, perhaps a word should be added about the use of the words "democracy" and "dictatorship." No attempt has been made to give democracy a precise definition. As Jean Jacques Rousseau pointed out in 1762, "If we take the term in its strictest sense, there never has been a real democracy, and there never will be. It is against the natural order for the many to govern and the few to be governed." [1] Both democracy and dictatorship are used in their popular meaning. The former means popular government and representative institutions, while dictatorship is used to convey the opposite idea or to describe the opposite type of government. Until recently dictatorship was used to convey the idea of the temporary possession by one man of unlimited power, a sort of trusteeship as in the constitution of the Roman Republic, to enable the state to weather a crisis. Nowadays crisis has become a permanent feature of society and the meaning of the word has changed. In this book common usage has been adopted, and the word dictatorship has been used as synonymous with autocracy or absolutism. The author considers the Soviet Union as well as the so-called "people's democracies" to be in fact dictatorships because the people are denied the right to free discussion and an opportunity to influence directly the policies of the government.

The literature has grown so large that it is impossible to give a complete or meaningful bibliography. Authors representative of the various points of view discussed are cited in the footnotes as well as those to whom I am particularly indebted. However, there is no other reason why these particular authors should be mentioned in preference to others.

The following publishers have kindly granted permission for quotations used in the text: Jonathan Cape, Ltd.; The Macmillan Company; Rinehart and Company, Inc.; McGraw-Hill Book Company, Inc.; Editor of *The Fortnightly;* Alfred A. Knopf, Inc.; University of North Carolina Press; W. W. Norton and Company, Inc.; Oxford University Press; Charles Scribner's Sons; Charles Scribner's Sons, Ltd.; Constable and Company, Ltd.; The American Political Science Association; The American Historical Association; University of Chicago Press; Ginn and Company; Longmans, Green and Company, Inc.; Cambridge University Press; Henry A. Kissinger, Editor of *Confluence;* The John Day Company, Inc.; Henry Holt and Company, Inc.; The Journal Press; New York University Press; George Allen and Unwin, Ltd.; W. Heffer and Sons, Ltd.; and Harcourt, Brace and Company, Inc.

It is impossible to acknowledge all of those who have contributed

1. *The Social Contract* (Everyman's Library; New York, 1935), Bk. III, Ch. iv, p. 58.

xii   *Preface*

directly or indirectly to the writing of this little volume. My former teachers at Yale University and my colleagues at Rutgers University have been the source of much inspiration and good advice. I am particularly indebted to Professors Cecil H. Driver and Francis W. Coker of the Department of Political Science at Yale University and to Professor E. M. Burns, Chairman of the Department of Political Science at Rutgers University. The author was privileged to read a portion of an unpublished manuscript on German political parties by Professor Louis W. Hallgring, Jr., a former colleague now in the Department of History at Hunter College. Finally and most important, I should like to express my appreciation to the Committee on International Relations at the University of Notre Dame for undertaking publication of the book. Members of the Committee generously gave their time and advice; and without these suggestions this volume would have been a much worse book than it is. I am particularly indebted to the Rev. Stanley J. Parry, C.S.C., Head of the Politics Department at Notre Dame, Professor Stephen D. Kertesz, Chairman of the Committee on International Relations, Professor Mathew A. Fitzsimons, Director of Publications for the Committee, and Professor Ferdinand A. Hermens, whose own work has been a source of inspiration and who discovered a number of errors in the manuscript. The work was completed much sooner than it otherwise could have been done because of generous grants from the Rutgers Research Council, the help of Messrs. John Anderegg and Seldon Kruger, graduate assistants in the Department of Political Science at Rutgers, and the aid and encouragement furnished by my wife. The conclusions reached are my own, and none of the individuals mentioned here are responsible for them.

N. L. S.

New Brunswick, New Jersey

CONTENTS

xiv *Contents*

Introduction

THE technical reasons why Professor Stamps's study is welcome are obvious. As the literature on the origin of dictatorships is both extensive and diffuse, his presentation of the various types of explanation advanced should be as much of a help to the general reader as it will be to the student of the subject. Both will be grateful for a degree of clarity and lucidity which is rarely reached in professional writing.

Considerations of principle constitute, however, an even stronger reason why this study is timely. Social scientists in general, and political scientists in particular, face the difficult task of holding their own in the face of the even more rapid advances made by the natural sciences, and of the destructive purposes which some of these advances have been made to serve in a politically disorganized world. For reasons frequently stated the task of the social scientist is, of course, harder than that of the natural scientist. A contributing factor is, however, frequently overlooked. Natural scientists constitute a true scientific community; they work in the closest possible contact, and the conclusions of one are constantly checked by others. Where errors creep in, they are not likely to persist. Political scientists, on the other hand, tend to work in isolation; they reach their conclusions independently of one another, and their writings, at times, assume the form of monologues in which everyone sets forth his own views, without much concern for what has been done by others. Even if this is done brilliantly it will not lead to that systematic sifting of the evidence without which generally accepted results cannot be secured. Besides, the striving for originality, so natural in itself, can be a sign of scientific immaturity; it implies that everything is constantly questioned, even the very foundations upon which our conclusions have to rest.

Professor Stamps has, therefore, done well in setting for himself the task of sifting the evidence, and the arguments, which others have presented; the systematic comparison at which he aims will make it a good deal easier to establish an effective dialogue, to register agreement where it is possible, and to identify the areas of disagreement where they can, as yet, not be eliminated. He would be the first to disclaim finality for every point he makes; the very nature of his approach calls for a continuation of the effort to establish more co-operation, and more mutual checking and auditing among political scientists than now exists. His views, too, need to be discussed and, where necessary, challenged, if the aim of an effective confrontation of opinions is to be reached. We might, to begin with, hold that the conclusions which the political scientist is able to reach are a little more definite than Professor Stamps assumes. Two centuries ago, Montesquieu wrote: "The Laws, in the widest meaning of the term, are the necessary relationships which follow from the nature of things." Perhaps we should dispense with the term "laws" altogether; it has engendered too many misunderstandings. Certainly, however, there do exist in political life "relationships which follow from the nature of things." If space permitted our discussing the matter in detail, our final conclusions would hardly be different from the way in which Alexander Hamilton concludes his examination of the subject in No. 31 of *The Federalist* papers:

> Though it cannot be pretended that the principles of moral and political knowledge have, in general, the same degree of certainty with those of the mathematics, yet they have much better claims in this respect than, to judge from the conduct of men in particular situations, we should be disposed to allow them. The obscurity is much oftener in the passions and prejudices of the reasoner than in the subject. Men, upon too many occasions, do not give their own understanding fair play; but, yielding to some untoward bias, they entangle themselves in words and confound themselves in subtleties.

If this is correct we can, with a reasonable hope of success, tackle the task of ascertaining in political life the "relationships which follow from the nature of things." To do so means not only that our understanding of the forces which move our world will be enhanced, but also that, when an opportunity presents itself for guiding these forces into constructive channels we shall not simply let it go by default.

The political scientist of our day is inclined to be frightened when confronted with such an evaluation of his potentialities. He would do well to consider the changes which one of his sister sciences, economics, has experienced in living memory. Thus, the end of the First World War witnessed inflations which, in several countries, reached the runaway stage. Their effects shattered social as well as economic life; even moral standards were affected and seemed, at times, as much debased as the currency. The political sphere did not enjoy immunity from this general disintegration. It was no accident that Mussolini seized power at a time when the effects of the Italian inflation had not yet worn off, and that Hitler's meteoric emergence from obscurity occurred, a year later, at the peak of the German inflation. Contrariwise, when the German currency was stabilized, a measure of stability returned to political life; both the Nazi and the Communist parties suffered reverses.

These runaway inflations did not have to occur. The factors which cause inflations were analyzed in detail by the "Bullion Committee," appointed in England to investigate why, in connection with the wars of the Napoleonic period, the price of gold bullion had risen. The majority of the committee agreed that the blame lay with the increase of the supply of money in relation to the supply of goods, and it identified the methods to be used to prevent such developments from arising, as well as to bring them under control once they had set in. Of the findings of this committee, the nineteenth century economist, Henry Dunning MacLeod wrote that they were as compelling as the demonstrations of Euclid. In our day, we might want to make some modifications in regard to the recommendations of the Bullion Committee, and add qualifications to their endorsement by MacLeod. Yet, had professional economists brought what was essential in these findings—won in a process of mutual checking so comparable to that of the natural sciences—to public attention with a modicum of emphasis, the necessary measures might, in several countries, have been taken before financial and social disruption had reached its peak.

Deflations can be as destructive as inflations. In the 1930's a continuous fall in the price level shook the foundations of economic, social and political stability in country after country. In Germany, the volume of Nazi and Communist votes increased in inverse proportion to the price level and in direct proportion to the rise of unemployment; by September 1930 a condition had been achieved in which the normal interplay of a democratic majority, and a democratic opposition, could no longer operate in the Reichstag. After that, it took little more than two years for Hitler to come to power. This was not a necessary result, to be sure; the chain of causation could have been broken by the proper type of action in the fields of either domestic or of foreign policy. Still, deflation and depression had set the stage on which these subsequent acts of commission and omission could become decisive. Nor was the situation, to mention just one more example, entirely different when the Japanese militarists displaced the proponents of parliamentary government from power; Japan, too, had been shaken deeply by the effects of the world economic crisis.

When the Second World War ended, it was widely expected that the Western world would, once again, find itself exposed to all the dangers resulting from inflationary and deflationary movements. The masters of the Kremlin, in particular, looked forward to a typical post-war depression in the United States. Not only did this depression fail to materialize, but the Western world has, in recent years, embarked upon a period of economic expansion which, while it is by no means free from tensions, has yet been strong enough to enhance our hopes that we can solve our problems in the framework of freedom.

In this development the science of economics has had its share. Whatever else may be said about the Keynesian revolution, (and there is no lack of economists who remain strongly critical of some of Keynes's major tenets), it did have the effect of raising the basic questions so insistently that they could no longer be ignored. As a result, professional economists did what they could to work as a true scientific community. In the meetings of the American Economic Association, for example, it is customary to pit a strong proponent of one view against an equally strong opponent; in the *American Economic Review,* critical notes remain an essential part of each issue. The clash of opinions and personalities continues. Still, among the vast majority of professional economists there is now agreement not only that inflationary and deflationary movements must not be allowed to exceed certain limits, but also, that there are adequate means for their control. Specifically, what the Council of Economic Advisors has proposed during the Eisenhower administration does not differ in essentials from what the majority of that body's members advocated during the concluding years of the Truman administration. Differences of degree and of emphasis remain; they had their repercussions during the 1956 presidential campaign. Yet, when President Eisenhower made it clear, as early as in 1953, that he would move with all the resources at the government's command, against deflation as well as against inflation, a measure of agreement became apparent for which few dared hope a generation ago.

Can political scientists achieve similar results? Can they, too, help to close the ring of measures needed to assure the success of democracy, and to forestall the rise of new dictatorships? It may perhaps be well to begin with a somewhat simpler classification of the factors responsible for the failure of democracy, and the rise of dictatorships, than is presented by Professor Stamps (who had to follow the tortuous path of the various explanations given in the literature of the subject). Aristotle's distinction between "form" and "matter" comes to hand. For the Greek philosopher "form" was not, as it is for most of us, the opposite, but an integral part, of "substance." When, for example, the sculptor sets out to create a statue, the block of marble is his "matter," and what he adds, aided by the proper tools, is the "form." Certainly, this process of forming is as vital, if the substance of statue is to be achieved as is the block of marble. On the other hand, of course, "matter" is equally important. Leave the sculptor with no more than a pile of dry sand and, even with the best of tools, he will be powerless. There exists, then, a mutual dependence between form and matter. Matter, in itself, is a mere potentiality; form, by itself, is without content.

All of this applies to the field of politics as much as to that of art, but with one major qualification. The "matter" of political life is human society which constitutes, in the language of the schoolmen, *materia secunda,* "secondary matter," rather than *materia prima,* "prime matter." Individual human beings have, to a considerable extent, been formed by a variety of social groups—the family, the churches, social classes, professional organizations—before the specific ingredients of political form obtain a chance to act on them.

To these social groups there applies, however, what John Locke had in mind when he spoke of the "variety of views and the contrariety of interests which unavoidably happen in all collections of men." The characteristic feature of society is, indeed, its divisiveness, and that of the state is unity—unity of action, primarily, and unity of thought to the extent that unity of action requires it. This transition from diversity to unity does not take place spontaneously; political form is the factor which stands between the two, acting, so to speak, as the transformer of society, creating, in the process, organs able to secure what St. Thomas Aquinas so aptly called "the unity of peace."

Political form, then, must always be present unless there is anarchy. This does not mean that any one type of political form can always succeed. If it does not conform to the needs of the social matter at hand, it will fail and be replaced by another. Professor Stamps deals with case after case where the political forms of democracy did fail; more often than not the reason lay in a type of social "matter" which lends itself with difficulty to the requirements of democratic form. If democracy is government based on the active consent of the governed (rather than the more passive type characteristic, for example, of "legitimate" monarchy) such government is hardly possible where illiteracy deprives the majority of the people—even in the days of radio and television—of reliable access to information concerning the activities of the government in regard to which they are supposed to express either consent or dissent. Whatever views are, under such conditions, declared to have been expressed by a majority carry but a limited moral weight. Besides, genuine freedom of elections is rare where widespread illiteracy exists, and it is rather much to expect a candidate to be a *good* loser when he has reason to doubt that he *was* the loser. The Latin American republics have, for well over a century, labored under these difficulties; at present, seventeen of the twenty-one live under one form of dictatorship or another.

Deficiencies of political form may, in fact, be as detrimental to democratic vitality as inadequate social material. To emphasize this factor means no more than to return to the principles enunciated by the founders of the American Republic. In 1777 Alexander Hamilton wrote in a letter to Gouverneur Morris:

That instability is inherent in the nature of popular governments I think very disputable; unstable democracy, is an epithet frequently in the mouths of politicians; but I believe that from a strict examination of the matter—from the records of history, it will be found that the fluctuations of governments in which the popular principle has borne a considerable sway, have proceeded from its being compounded with other principles;—*and from its being made to operate in an improper channel.*

Hamilton was not alone in believing that serious damage could be done to democratic government by "its being made to operate in an improper channel." This thought was basic to all of those who had a share in the framing of the new constitution. Thus, Madison, speaking in No. 48 of *The Federalist* of certain evils occurring in the course of the "critical period of American history" commented: "Some of them, it will be found, may be imputable to peculiar circumstances connected with the war; but the greater part of them may be considered as *the spontaneous shoots of an ill-constituted government.*" (Italics supplied.) Finally, Madison, in No. 10 of *The Federalist,* dealing with the detrimental results of mob psychology which the annals of history record with such distressing frequency in "pure democracies" where a popular assembly of thousands of unorganized citizens makes vital decisions, says that they *"result from the form of government itself."* (Italics supplied.)

It was the argument of the proponents of the constitution, including, at an early date, George Washington, that many of the trials which they encountered derived, indeed, from "the form of government itself." The potential strength of the people was as great under the Articles of Confederation as it was later under the Constitution, but the Articles made it impossible to actualize it. There was, in fact, no lack of learned observers who argued that nothing could be done; on that vast continent, they held, there existed such a basic heterogeneity that the people could not possibly live under one government. Nor was there a lack of counsels of despair, some of George Washington's officers, in a famous incident, believing that they were serving their country by offering to make him king and conferring titles of nobility upon a number of army officers. Colonel Nicola's plan was, to be sure, more moderate, and a great deal more democratic than appears from reading only the stern reproof administered to him by George Washington, which is nearly all that most historians dealing with the incident relate. Still, Washington was right in his uncompromising opposition to the proposal as the interpretation on which it rested would, in this case as in others, have made a bad political situation infinitely worse. Had the plan been acted upon, there would have been another failure of democracy to explain; the case would have been fully parallel to those discussed in this book because, in a country where the leaven of democracy has been at work as much as it had been on these shores, even at that time, the alternative to a faltering democracy is a dictatorship rather than a constitutional monarchy with a chance of becoming "legitimate" in the sense given to that term by Guglielmo Ferrero.

A different result was achieved by establishing, first of all, intellectual clarity within what was a comparatively small, but influential, group, and then trying, again and again, to bring about the necessary reforms. Success seemed, for years, out of reach; Hamilton's "Letters from Phokion" are indicative of the mood of despair which pervaded the leaders of the country for some time. Still, as long as these men knew what they wanted they were certain not to allow any opportunity for action to pass which might present itself; the result was the Federal Constitution. It was limited to a change in political form; the country, with all its social and economic problems, remained the same. Still, in short order, the new nation developed a vigor contrasting sharply with the paralysis prevailing under the Articles of Confederation. One is reminded of Aristotle who in the fourth chapter of the third book of his *Politics* said that "when the form of government changes, and becomes different, then it may be supposed that the state is no longer the same." This is, indeed, what happened in the United States when "improper channels" of political action were replaced by the proper ones.

The trend of thought which guided the framers of the Constitution is more directly applicable to a discussion of the reasons for the rise of modern dictatorships than appears at first glance. Madison's discussion of "factions" in No. 10 of *The Federalist* covers all possible elements of social division; his catalogue is, indeed, not limited to those arising from economic cleavages, as Charles A. Beard seemed to believe in his younger days, and made so many others believe. Madison placed emphasis on passion—at present we might say fanaticism—as well as on economic interests. Much of what he says about factions fits modern totalitarian parties as if it had been written for them. Professor Stamps rightly remarks that these groups are essentially different from democratic parties. The question is how to meet the threat arising from their existence without jeopardizing the freedom which we want to defend against them; it is exactly the question which Madison set out to answer. In the very first sentence of his essay he states it as his purpose to look for ways to "break and control the violence of faction" without endangering freedom. Of the safeguards on which they rely majority rule is the first:

> If a faction consists of less than a majority, relief is supplied by the republican principle, which enables the majority to defeat its sinister views by regular vote. It may clog the administration, it may convulse the society; but it will be unable to execute and mask its violence under the forms of the Constitution.

For Madison, then, it is obvious that violent minorities must not be introduced into the central organs of democratic government, allowing them to proceed to do their destructive work from within. That this must be done is, however, a contention advanced, for over a century, by the proponents of proportional representation (P.R.) even if not all of them were as explicit as one of their major theoreticians, Victor Considérant, who demanded that "all opinions, even the most absurd and the most monstrous ones, must have their representatives in parliament in a number proportional to their strength in the electorate." The events of the last generation have given ample proof where such a practice leads.

The analysis of the part played by political form in the weakness of democratic government must, of course, let it be repeated, always be supplemented by the analysis of the part played by social "matter." It is, however, important to bear in mind that where the pre-political conditions for the success of democratic government are largely absent, it still makes a difference whether this material is cast into the "proper," or into the improper "channels of government." The best example is India, where the basic heterogeneity of racial, social and religious life is greater than anywhere else, where illiteracy covers 80 per cent of the population, and where the number of the unemployed has been put at 30 million. Any one of these handicaps could be fatal to the operation of democratic government;

in their combination they are staggering. The Indian constitution, however, burdened as it is with unnecessary detail, does attempt to face these problems with a coherent political action-pattern—that of a parliamentary system supplemented by the plurality system of voting. The latter was deliberately chosen for the purpose of encouraging the various elements of the population to merge on the basis of common citizenship—to establish a basis for consent where P.R. would have been bound to register nothing but dissent. In the elections of 1951–52 the Congress Party, which does aim at a broad consensus of all social, religious and racial groups, with a little less than 45 per cent of the votes, secured 74 per cent of the seats. Such a result is not ideal, in particular since it does not entail the growth of a democratic opposition which could take the burden of responsibility off the Congress Party's shoulders if it should falter. Still, a constructive force emerged, and it was given the tools it needed to attack the age-old evils of Indian society. It did so with a variety of measures, including the two five-year plans. The first one took several years to catch fire, but it did so in the end. At present, the prospects for Indian democracy—bound to be highly uncertain for decades, if not generations—are perceptibly brighter than they were but a few years ago.

If the analysis of the reasons for the weakness betrayed by democratic government indicated in these few lines is correct, we shall no longer speak just of *the* failure of democracy. We shall, instead, be on the lookout for a variety of specific factors which have, in a particular historical setting, weakened and, at times, destroyed democratic government. None of them may be easy to remedy. If defects in the political structure are to blame, their correction presupposes a struggle with the confusionists first, and the "vested interests" second; neither is readily won. If there are deficiencies in the social "matter," the issue may be even more complex, and an entire "strategy for development" may be needed. It can, however, be devised. There is, perhaps, no better example than the *Report on Cuba,* prepared for the International Bank for Reconstruction and Development in collaboration with the government of Cuba. It clearly outlines—on more than 1000 pages—not only the complexity of the problem, but also the various steps which can be taken, in order to attack them; some of them, in fact, are now in the process of being taken. What was done so well in this case can be done in others, even if political analysis has much to do to catch up with economic analysis. At any rate, to the extent that we manage to ascertain the nature of the concrete factors involved in a given country in the weakness of democratic government, we create the possibility of taking advantage of such opportunities for remedial action as may present themselves.

Any hesitation to undertake so complicated and, at times, frustrating a task should be dispelled by the simple consideration that if democracy failed in a number of instances, dictatorship *always* fails. Aristotle termed it the least stable form of government and, in our day, we have seen dictatorships disintegrating repeatedly, leaving democracy to pick up the pieces. It is interesting to note that a writer as little favorable to democracy as Oswald Spengler has this to say on the subject:

> By the term 'Caesarism' I mean that kind of government which, irrespective of any constitutional formulation that it may have, is in its inward self a return to thorough formlessness . . . It does not matter that Augustus in Rome, and Hwang-ti in China, Amasis in Egypt and Alp Arslan in Baghdad disguised their position under antique forms. The spirit of these forms was dead, and so all institutions, however carefully maintained, were thenceforth destitute of all meaning and weight. Real importance centred in the wholly personal power exercised by the Caesar, or by anybody else capable of exercising it in his place. It is the *recidive* of a form-fulfilled world into primitivism, into the cosmichistoryless. Biological stretches of time once more take the place vacated by historical periods.

What the author of *The Decline of the West* says about "Caesarism" is basically true for all dictatorships. They all entail a denial of true form. Latin American writers bring out this fact when they distinguish between what they call "institutionalism" and "personalism." Institutionalism, the essence of true political form, assures stability; when, for example, in the United States a president dies, the vice-president succeeds him within a matter of hours; when, in Britain, a Churchill is defeated, the leader of the Labor Party may appear in Buckingham Palace within the hour in order to receive the seals of office. This subordination of the person under the institution is the only possible guarantee for stability. Where, however, as in a dictatorship, the person is bigger than the institution, the death or removal of the man at the top means a deep and prolonged crisis, often followed by the end of the system.

A proper functioning of democracy is free from dependence upon persons. Even where democratic government fails it is interesting to note that, after a more or less extended interval of dictatorship, the attempt is made to restore it. People will grope for it; they may struggle for it heroically as did the people of Hungary in the last months of 1956. Evidently it represents a condition of stable equilibrium, and dictatorship a condition of unstable equilibrium. The analysis bound to precede it can benefit greatly from the fact that Professor Stamps's conclusions may well be accepted as final in regard to at least two of the various types of explanation with which he deals. What he says in regard to the psychological, and the (exclusively) economic interpretation of the reasons why democracies have failed is distinguished both by sound reasoning and brilliant exposition. Henceforth, the task of the social analyst will be simplified if, in accordance with Professor Stamps's suggestion, he discards these two interpretations, even though they are as fashionable in certain circles as they are untenable.

FERDINAND A. HERMENS

University of Notre Dame
February, 1957

THE FAILURE OF DEMOCRACY

AT THE end of World War I it appeared as though democracy had reached its greatest triumph. Lord Bryce in his *Modern Democracies,* first published in 1921, pointed out that "A century ago there was in the Old World only one tiny spot in which the working of democracy could be studied." [1] This was in "a few of the ancient rural cantons of Switzerland" but "nowhere else in Europe did the people rule." However, within a hundred years "nearly all the monarchies of the Old World have been turned into democracies," twenty new republics have sprung up in the Western hemisphere, and five new democracies developed out of colonies within the British dominions. Lord Bryce added that more than a hundred representative assemblies were at work legislating for self-governing communities but that the most significant change in the last hundred years was "the universal acceptance of democracy as the normal and natural form of government." The word, democracy, which had formerly awakened dislike or fear, was now a word of praise; and the old question as to what is the best form of government had become almost obsolete. [2]

THE CLIMAX OF "CLASSIC CONSTITUTIONALISM"

This almost universal confidence in the ultimate triumph of popular government was not merely the mood of this generation but was

1. James Bryce, *Modern Democracies* (New York, 1924), I, 3.
2. *Ibid.,* pp. 3–4.

1

instead the climax of an ever-widening and deepening conviction that democracy was the predestined form of government for all civilized nations. Jeremy Bentham, James and John Stuart Mill, Thomas Paine, and Thomas Jefferson believed that, given widespread educational opportunities, the whole world would eventually become democratic.

The revolt of the American colonies, the teachings of the French philosophers, the contagion of the French Revolution, the Reform Acts of 1832, 1867, and 1884 in Britain, as well as other political developments in the nineteenth century, seemed to support the view that there is a linear pattern of advance from absolutism along democratic lines and that it was possible to predict the path which governments would follow. Everywhere it appeared as though democratic institutions were spreading from the countries most advanced in economic and political development to those states whose evolution, even if retarded, was proceeding in the same direction. Even W. E. H. Lecky, whose own misgivings concerning democracy effectively protected him against any suspicion of wishful thinking, wrote in 1896:

> I do not think that anyone who seriously considers the force and universality of the movement of our generation in the direction of democracy can doubt that this conception of government will necessarily, at least for a considerable time, dominate in all civilized countries, and the real question for politicians is the form it is likely to take, and the means by which its characteristic evils can be best mitigated.[3]

The World War increased, rather than diminished, belief in the irresistible triumph of popular government. Woodrow Wilson gradually became convinced that the selfish ambition of irresponsible kings and military rulers was a major cause of the conflict. When America entered the war the absolute Tsarist regime in Russia had been replaced by a provisional government committed to the selection of a constituent assembly, and Wilson announced in his message to Congress that a major aim of the allied cause was to "make the world safe for democracy." At the end of the war military defeat had brought an end to the reign, not only of the Romanov, but also to the Hapsburg and Hohenzollern dynasties; and the victory of the Entente powers was attributed partially to the democratic spirit

3. William Edward Hartpole Lecky, *Democracy and Liberty* (New York, 1913), I, 256.

of their peoples. Thus the return of peace coincided with the establishment of democratic constitutions all over Europe.

THE RUDE AWAKENING

It was hardly expected that a rapid spread of dictatorship should begin at this time; yet there were signs of approaching danger. The victory of the allied powers had been possible after the temporary suspension of civil liberties and the concentration of practically unlimited powers in the executive. In order to provide efficiency and the aim and direction necessary to win the war, representative assemblies in England, France, and the United States abandoned their peace time authority. A strict censorship made it impossible for public opinion to assert itself or become sufficiently enlightened to exercise an intelligent choice. Information was supplied almost entirely by government propaganda offices, and hence the normal working of free institutions was impossible. "The conflict," as Keith Hutchison has said, "absorbed so large a proportion of the national resources that the State was forced to develop a war economy on socialist lines and, although the measures adopted were regarded as 'for the duration' only, important administrative and psychological residues remained after the peace." [4]

A few close students of government noted that the universal acceptance of democracy was not a tribute to the smoothness of its working and that discontent was everywhere rife. For example, Lord Bryce, writing in 1921, concluded that there were few countries "in which freedom seems safe for a century or two ahead"; [5] but such statements were exceptional at this time. Although a provisional government committed to the election of a constituent assembly had triumphed over Russian Tsarism in March, 1917, a Communist dictatorship of the proletariat under Lenin soon took its place. In 1922 Mussolini made his famous "march on Rome" and

4. *The Decline and Fall of British Capitalism* (New York, 1950), p. 133.
5. *Modern Democracies* (1921), II, 603. For a discussion of the constitutions adopted after World War I, see Agnes Headlam-Morley, *The New Democratic Constitutions of Europe* (London, 1929). In 1913 A. Lawrence Lowell had written: "Many people feel that because popular government is new it must be lasting. They know it is a vital part of the spirit of the age, which they assume to be permanent. But that is the one thing the spirit of the age never is. It would not deserve its name if it were; and when any spirit of the age has become universally recognized, it is time to scan the horizon for signs of a new era." *Public Opinion and Popular Government* (New York, 1913), p. 303.

began the gradual consolidation of power which was eventually to turn Italy into a totalitarian state. However, defenders of democracy, for the most part, were undisturbed by these developments. It was explained that party government had never taken root in Italy or Russia and that these countries had merely turned from one form of dictatorship to another.

In the years that followed, the collapse of parliamentary institutions continued. By 1933 not only were great powers, such as Russia, Italy, and Germany, ruled by dictatorial regimes; but some form of dictatorship had been adopted in the smaller nations as well. One author, writing in 1935, described the situation as follows:

> The reaction against post-war democracy was violent and almost universal. To recall the chronological progress of dictatorship since the War: Russia in 1918, Hungary in 1919, Turkey after 1920, Italy after 1922, Portugal in 1925, Poland after 1926, Yugoslavia in 1929, Germany in 1933, Austria, Estonia, and Bulgaria in 1934, adopted a form of dictatorial government which, despite some ideological and circumstantial differences, shows a striking similarity in governmental technique.
>
> Scarcely two decades ago, discussion ran high over the value of monarchy; parliamentary democracy appeared as the inescapable solution. At present, democracy is everywhere on the defensive, and the victory of autocracy seems hardly less inevitable than formerly the universal acceptance of democracy. Fear persists more than ever that the contagious spread of dictatorships cannot be checked.[6]

As a matter of fact, this list of European countries under some form of dictatorship was far from complete even at the time when Professor Loewenstein wrote. In addition to the states he mentioned as having adopted an authoritarian regime, Albania, Rumania, Latvia, and Lithuania could also have been added.[7] Events after 1935 show a further decline in parliamentary institutions and a further spread of autocracy. Prior to the overthrow of monarchy in Spain, there was a military dictatorship under General Primo de Rivera. Although a republican form of government and a liberal constitution were adopted after the revolution in 1931, political

6. Karl Loewenstein, "Autocracy versus Democracy in Contemporary Europe," *The American Political Science Review*, XXIX (1935), 574.

7. Maurice Parmelee, *Bolshevism, Fascism and the Liberal-Democratic State* (New York, 1934), pp. 4–5; Joseph R. Starr, "The Chronology of Dictatorship in Post-War Europe," in Guy Stanton Ford (ed.), *Dictatorship in the Modern World* (Minneapolis, 1939), pp. 331–362. A summary of political events in each of these countries can be found in the annual issues of the *Political Handbook of the World*.

conditions remained unsettled until 1936 when the Spanish civil war broke out which resulted in General Francisco Franco emerging as the head of a new military dictatorship. It was in 1936 also that General John Metaxas advised the king to suspend the Greek constitution and brought that country, which has had an unusually turbulent political history, once more under dictatorial rule. By 1938 all of central and eastern Europe and all Mediterranean countries were under dictatorial rule.

EFFECT ON THE STUDY OF GOVERNMENT

This experience has compelled us to reopen our method of studying politics and develop a new frame of reference. The old corpus of analysis taught in the standard text books drew its conclusions from the experience of Great Britain, the United States, France, Canada, Australia, and the Scandinavian countries. Many countries obviously didn't fit into this method of analysis; and when they didn't fit, we tended to treat them as a problem. Thus there was "the German problem," "the problem of Mussolini and Italy," the Russian Communists, and Pilsudski in Poland. In other words, our tradition and system of analysis has taken care of the democratic world; but it was shocked at what it saw elsewhere and has been unable to "explain" dictatorships within the terms of its own technique of analysis. We are faced with the task of working out a new system of analysis to take care of the non-democratic world.

During the last few years an increasing number of political scientists, sociologists, economists, and psychologists have become interested in this task; and there is already a great deal of literature in the field. However, most writers have been interested in developing a particular thesis or a single explanation; and no one as yet has attempted to survey the work that has been done, analyze it, and bring together in a single book the results obtained thus far.

EVOLUTION OF THE
MODERN NATION STATE

IN RECENT years there has been an increasing awareness that the study of government should concern itself, not merely with structure and the "form of constitutions," but also with the nature and character of our civilization and its impact on governments. This has been an outgrowth of an earlier realization that government is a cultural phenomenon, that there are few "laws" governing political behavior, and that a profitable study of government can be undertaken only in this larger cultural context. Although political science has erred in failing to take this fact sufficiently into account, it is equally wrong to assume that the "form of constitutions" is of no importance.[1] Thus all constitutions are the result of experience and tradition, but they are also molded and shaped continuously by the forces present in a given society. Institutions are not static and permanent; on the other hand, Burke was right in seeing them as the result of a long history of development and the product of "the accumulated wisdom of the ages."

EMERGENCE OF THE MODERN NATION STATE

Throughout history man has lived under many different kinds of public organization. First, there was the tribe which has survived

1. For a brief but important discussion of this subject, see F. A. Hermens, "Politics and Ethics," *Thought*, XXIX (1954), 32–50.

6

in large areas of the world today. Then came the village; the ancient empires, which were largely theocratic and static; the *polis* or city-state; and the imperium first of Macedonia and then of Rome. The next stage was feudalism which is a recurring phenomenon in history and which has often appeared when a preceding civilization was destroyed.

After the division of the Roman Empire there was a period of chaos in the West. The continual disorder, together with the most primitive means of communication, made it impossible for the central government to protect life and property, and hence the small landowner or the man of small power became dependent upon someone strong enough to aid him. "Feudalism," Professor McIlwain tells us, "is properly nothing more than a general name for the common features of many diverse local institutions." [2] It was an amalgam of the tribal organization of the Teutons with the organization of Rome. Society was organized by a vast network of personal contractual obligations with individuals having concrete rights and with the feudal domain as the unit of political organization. Most of the functions considered as public today were private in the middle ages. Although there was great diversity, some of the larger feudal domains gained the right to administer justice, developed their own legal systems, and were practically independent. If the king tried to take over functions exercised by his vassals, he was certain to face strong opposition. Sometimes, as in the case of Magna Carta, the nobles forced the king to promise not to interfere with their private rights. In any case, the splintering of authority led to a long period of civil war during which a large number of little men became a small number of greater men and out of which came a craving on the part of people generally for peace and order.

The result was that the king gathered into his own hands the authority which had been dispersed and a new type of public organization—the modern nation state—came into being. As a matter of fact, the origin of the word "state" demonstrates what happened. The Romans had used *"res publica,"* and Machiavelli is reported to have first used the term *lo stato* in *The Prince* published in 1513. In the middle ages the term status, estate, or state indi-

2. C. H. McIlwain, *The Growth of Political Thought in the West* (New York, 1932), p. 180.

cated standing or position. One could have standing or position in respect to land (an estate), to membership in a class (estates of the realm), or to authority. Thus there was a royal estate, an ecclesiastical estate, and so on. During this period the royal estate became supreme or identical with the state. The king's secretaries were first called secretaries of the royal estate and later secretaries of state.

The attainment of unity was aided by the growth of nationalism, but unification also evoked a spontaneous feeling of pride which gave forth the spirit of nationalism. There was a revival in the study of Roman law, and these "Roman lawyers" played an important part in helping form the new monarchy. The new middle class furnished most of the advisers and helped make up the new bureaucracy. As a matter of fact, they had played a leading role in the formation of the absolutist state. Civil war and chaos were bad for business, and hence the bourgeoisie financed the king's efforts to bring about peace and order. The absolutist state was not merely imposed by force. A social and political system can seldom be achieved in this way. Britain, France, and Spain were the first states to evolve, for unification in Italy and Germany was not experienced until about 1870. As a matter of fact, the Rhine was the dividing line in this process, for in central Europe the feudal lords were never completely brought under control. Instead each one tried to make himself absolute in his own small domain. Therefore, when unification was finally achieved, it was only a partial unity because the disintegrating influence of particularism and localism remained. What happened in Britain in the sixteenth century did not occur in Germany and Italy until the nineteenth century, and hence these two countries today are in many ways psychologically contemporary with Britain at the time of Elizabeth.[3]

Major Phases of the Modern Nation State

Social evolution has gone on continuously, and the modern nation state, once it came into being, has itself undergone an evolu-

3. Professor Carl J. Friedrich, *Constitutional Government and Democracy* (revised edition; New York, 1950), p. 25, says that "from the standpoint of economic and constitutional development, Cecil, Colbert, and Frederick William I are 'contemporaries.' Although one worked in the sixteenth, one in the seventeenth, and one in the eighteenth century, they were each responsible for consolidating one of the modern power systems. They were each responsible likewise for consolidating an administrative service, a bureaucracy, which a succeeding generation could then subject to controls and thus convert into a constitutional system."

tion. In the beginning the emphasis was on unity because of the reaction against civil war. The most common philosophy in support of the new monarchy was the divine right of kings, but Hobbes attempted to give the system a rational basis. In any case, the emphasis was on strength; and there was a tendency to assert that "the will of the sovereign has the force of law." Strong executive power was a necessity at this time. Society was organized on a pyramidal basis with each person finding his proper place. On the economic side, the prevailing philosophy was mercantilism with its price-fixing and other controls. In other words, according to official theory the community was viewed as a unit, and the emphasis on uniformity meant that no deviation could be permitted. Hence there must be one church and one political ideology. In many countries this concept has lasted down to our own day.

The longer peace lasted and the more prosperous states became, the more people began to demand "freedom from" controls and the right to "participate in" government. These demands were spearheaded by the bourgeoisie, and thus the same class that had previously made absolute monarchy were now the men who broke it. Eventually men like John Milton, John Locke, Adam Smith, Jeremy Bentham, James and John Stuart Mill won out, and a new society was created.

Nineteenth century liberal democracy and *laissez-faire* economics were based upon a conception of the universe as a mechanism operating in accordance with natural laws. This principle was reinforced by the doctrine of the harmony of interests. Thus individuals by pursuing their own interests best served those of the community; an abundant supply of commodities at a fair and reasonable price was automatically taken care of by the operations of the market; and the function of government was to permit to these economic "laws" complete freedom of action. Such a conception accepted individual profit as the test of what is socially useful; and since it also denied the need of conscious and deliberate planning, it dispensed with any consideration of moral purpose other than individual self-interest.

Although liberalism has been widely proclaimed as essentially a bourgeois movement, it is important to note that a victory could not have been won fought on behalf of narrow middle class interests alone. The aristocratic privileges, so effectively denounced by the philosophers, were real enough; and all the unprivileged, bourgeois and people alike, had an interest in resisting them. In proclaiming the worth and dignity of the individual, bourgeois spokesmen were appealing to interests transcending all class lines. Freedom of economic enterprise was not stressed in the revolutionary propaganda nearly so much as the liberty of person and of opinion. The demand for freedom of religion and freedom of speech and press found widespread support among all classes. Moreover, freedom in the economic realm was needed at the time to emancipate industry from the restraints of monopolistic privilege and petty governmental regulations.

The nineteenth century was also an age of constitution-making. In order to maintain themselves kings conceded or granted written constitutions; and in many countries constituent assemblies drew up fundamental laws for the people. In these constitutions emphasis was placed upon a weak executive, and there was a tendency to divide powers. Nearly all of them contained a Bill of Rights. They tended to be negative and political in content: negative in the sense that they stated what the government may not do; and political in the sense that they defined who may participate in government. Most of these constitutions were copied from Britain, but the copying was extremely superficial. Walter Bagehot's *The English Constitution,* which was the first book to describe the British constitution accurately in terms of the way in which it operated, was not published until 1867; and hence the actual functioning of British institutions was not fully understood, either at home or abroad, until much later. Moreover, in every constitution certain moral and cultural conditions are presupposed and cannot be copied because they are a part of a people's heritage and are unconsciously accepted and obeyed. Hence many of the constitutions, which were modelled upon the system in Great Britain, worked very unsatisfactorily in their new environment.

Towards the end of the nineteenth century it became increasingly evident that the prevailing conception of society no longer accurately described the real situation nor did it provide a solution for a multitude of problems brought about by changing circumstances. For example, it became increasingly obvious that the law of supply and demand did not always secure an equitable and fair distribution of goods, that the growth of monopoly tended to stifle competition, and that the development of large-scale industry required the investment of huge sums in fixed capital assets which could not readily be shifted to other means of production. The emancipation of the individual from governmental restraint in his economic activities created new oppressions so that liberty for the majority of men could be achieved only by an extension of governmental regulation and control over business enterprise. Instead of individuals competing with one another, society more and more became a contest between organized interest groups. Unemployment and recurring economic crises created a feeling of insecurity among the masses, and they began to demand positive action on the part of government to provide minimum guarantees. The trend in the social service phase of the modern nation state is towards the substitution of welfare for the profit motive. Typical examples of the early demands on the state were for free public education, limitation of the hours of work, and workmen's compensation laws; but today they have been extended to include free medical care, old age insurance, unemployment compensation, and many other services as well.

Constitution-making in the social service phase of the modern state began at the end of World War I. These constitutions differed from those of the nineteenth century in that they were positive rather than negative and contained social and economic guarantees.[4] The preceding age was characterized by small business which it was impossible to regulate, but the new age is characterized by big business, big unions, and organized professional classes. In other words, the trend is away from atomic democracy, and the individual is replaced by the group. Many of the constitutions framed in this period emphasized the functional element of society. For example, the Weimar Constitution provided for an economic council separate from and independent of the regular parliament, and the Constitution of the Fourth French Republic also established an advisory economic council.

SIGNIFICANCE OF THIS DEVELOPMENT

A constitution cannot be considered simply from the point of view of machinery. The peculiar experiences of a people throughout the centuries molds its character in much the same way as an

4. For a discussion, see Agnes Headlam-Morley, *The New Democratic Constitutions of Europe* (London, 1929). It has sometimes been pointed out that these constitutions were more often declamatory than positive in character; but even though social and economic guarantees were generally unenforceable, they do illustrate the changed philosophy indicated in the text.

individual's personality is influenced by experience. Common experience creates in the nation common standards of value, common emotional reactions, and a peculiar sense of duty and responsibility that is absent in other communities not sharing in the same tradition. Thus the evolution of the modern nation state may be shown to have proceeded at a different pace in the different countries of the world, sometimes accelerated and sometimes retarded in any particular country because of differences in the psychology of the peoples involved as well as because of certain material factors; and the different experiences thus created have in turn produced an entirely different outlook on life.

Each phase of development creates institutions, which have as their objective the maintenance of that system, and a public psychology which makes these institutions possible. Political ideas always have a long history; they are handed down from generation to generation; and hence may be modified only very gradually and slightly. For the most part, men live within the framework of institutions that are not of their choosing. They are born into an established order that molds their minds and determines what they shall think and how they shall feel in a multitude of ways of which, for the most part, they are not even aware. When men's minds are cast in a particular mold for centuries, a peculiar cultural tradition is developed which may take an equally long time to disappear. An attempt to establish democracy by merely destroying the top symbols of the absolute dynastic state is foolish. Although the Kaiser was deposed and Germany was rid of the Hohenzollerns, there appears to have been no great change in the underlying psychological pattern which had developed in the German people. In this connection it is interesting to note that in Hungary Admiral Horthy was regent of a crown that did not exist and also admiral of a navy that did not exist. As Leonard Woolf has pointed out, this "psychological law of the dead hand" or "tyranny of the dead mind" explains why the living, who are making history, think dead men's thoughts, pursue dead men's ideals, even though the ideals themselves may be "dead and rotten" and "the mere ghosts of beliefs, ideals from which time has sapped all substance and meaning." [5] This tendency of men to accept the ideals of the past is important, not only because it gives rise to a

5. Leonard Woolf, *After the Deluge* (London, 1931), I, 33.

host of presuppositions that place definite limits upon our thinking, but also because it gives a stability and continuity without which society could not exist.

At the same time, though it may seem paradoxical, no social system is able to endure unless it remains forever susceptible to change and prepared at all times to modify its institutions and practices to meet the demands of fresh ideas, new techniques, and altered circumstances. Therefore, although all political and social ideals have a long history and are handed down from generation to generation, the symbols gradually take on new meaning as they come into contact with different circumstances and different ideas. Thus the radical notions of 1789 have now become a part of a conservative and respectable tradition. The ideals of freedom and liberty may have their origin in nineteenth century liberalism; but no nineteenth century liberal would recognize these words today as used by the Prime Minister of Great Britain, the Premier of Russia, the President of the United States, or the Chancellor of Germany; nor do freedom and liberty mean exactly the same thing to any two of these men. In other words, the ideals that govern the thinking of society at any given time and place are always changing; for although ideals, arising out of the wants of the past, become transformed and continue into the present, they gradually take on new meaning as they come into contact with different circumstances and different ideas.

The past is never completely obliterated, and hence ideas carried over from each of the preceding types of public organization are with us today. Thus institutions born in the past continue into the present and perpetuate their traditions. For example, there is the highly selective educational system in Britain which trains public servants and perpetuates the idea of training the ruling classes. Frederick the Great allowed all classes to enter the Prussian civil service, and thus it became the expression of hope and opportunity to many people. This fact partially explains why the civil service is so much admired in Germany, while the very word bureaucracy is a term of abuse in England and the United States. In any case, the civil service in Germany born in a period of absolutism has gone on generating its own ideology which is inimical to democracy to this very day.

Governments in the modern world do not represent the summation or climax of the long series of evolutionary changes, but instead reflect the different phases of each stage in the series. Millions in the world today still live under the tribal form; Abyssinia is still feudal; and although the modern nation state emerged in Britain in the sixteenth century, it did not come to Germany until the nineteenth century. Moreover, once the modern nation state came into existence, its evolution was different in the various countries of the world. In Britain, the integral phase, or the absolutist stage, gave way to a long liberal or *laissez-faire* period; and the nation was able to assume gradually the problems connected with the social service state. On the other hand, Germany went directly from the integral phase into the social service stage without ever experiencing the liberal period at all. As to whether those countries in which the liberal period lasted longest are better able to solve the problems of the social service state and maintain at the same time a democratic structure will be discussed in another chapter. In any case, the question arises as to whether it is possible to bring people from one of the older patterns to a more modern pattern, passing over thousands of years of development and experience, and still refrain from adopting a dictatorial government.

If the interpretation given here is correct, the world is likely to experience for sometime the coexistence of different types of democratic and dictatorial governments. The successful operation of democratic government can be achieved only through a long hard process of education and experience by which the taste and practice of self-rule are gradually acquired. In India representative government appears to have enjoyed a certain measure of success; but the principles of the Constitution have not yet penetrated society very deeply, and it would be a bold prophet who would claim that a stable foundation has been built. It may be that India has a better chance to avoid dictatorship than many other new nations emerging from colonial rule, partly because of her own traditions and partly because of the heritage of British ideas and practices; but the eventual success of democracy in that country depends to a great extent upon the ability of political leaders to reconcile cultural diversity with national unity and to encourage the development of a new set of social conventions which will overcome present distinctions of race, caste, creed, and economic opportunity. Democracy requires a sense of responsibility and a confidence on the part of citizens in their ability to govern themselves. "Such practice, however, is not encouraged in many parts of the world and is made more difficult by the tremendous differences in cultural levels and achievements in a world which embraces all types of civilizations, from the near-Neanderthal men of the Australian bush to the industrial men of the West." [6]

6. Robert G. Neumann, *European and Comparative Government* (Second edition; New York, 1955), p. 639.

Chapter 3

CLASSIFICATION

OF DICTATORSHIPS

THE traditional classification of governments, which has come down to us from antiquity, is based upon the number of people who participate in the government. For example, Aristotle distinguished between the "government of the few" and the "government of the many" and divided existing governments into the three "good" forms of monarchy, aristocracy, and "polity." He then described the perversions of these types into tyranny, oligarchy, and democracy. By "polity" Aristotle apparently meant a constitutional, middle-class government in which the many participate as distinguished from "democracy," by which he meant mob rule.[1]

Whatever the usefulness of this classification may have been in the past, it is meaningless for us today because it does not tell us anything significant about the governments so classified. There are absolute and limited monarchies, and there are republics which are federal and unitary, presidential and parliamentary, autocratic and popular. It is the reality, rather than the form of the constitution, which provides the basis for classification. For example, Fascist Italy was a party dictatorship even though it maintained a

1. Aristotle, *Politics,* Book IV, 1289a, b. Aristotle's classification follows Plato very closely. See *The Republic,* Books VIII and IX and also *The Statesman* where Plato distinguishes between the three types of law-abiding states (monarchy, aristocracy, and moderate or constitutional democracy) and the three types of arbitrary states (tyranny, oligarchy, and extreme democracy).

monarchical façade. Likewise Nazi Germany and Communist Russia are party dictatorships even though they technically could be classified as republics. Modern sociologists have clearly shown that nowhere in the world do "the people" rule but that in all states the exercise of government is left to a few hands.[2] As Professor Robert Neumann has pointed out, "The British cabinet rules the country for all practical purposes, and the same could be said about the Politburo in Moscow, yet nobody with any critical faculty would say that these two regimes are alike."[3] It is the relationship of a people to their government and the spirit of that government which count, and this involves a detailed study of its ideals, institutions, methods, practices, and policies.

DIFFICULTY OF CLASSIFICATION

It is obvious that many different and meaningful classifications of governments are possible and that the arrangement of governments in the world today into a short and simple classification is an impossible task. Any number of criteria present themselves as a possible basis for classification. For example, economic development could be used with the different areas of the world arranged according to primitive types, feudal arrangements, capitalist, and socialist forms. The type of community might also be used beginning with tribal government and ending with the dream of world government. Likewise the location and distribution of sovereignty, involving a consideration of unitary and federal forms, is another possibility as well as the more common method of using the constitutional basis for classification.[4] To place governments in their proper classification one must know them thoroughly, and when that is done, it will appear that there are about as many classes as there are governments.

2. R. M. MacIver, *The Web of Government* (New York, 1951), p. 149.
3. Robert G. Neumann, *European and Comparative Government* (New York, 1951), p. 575.
4. For a discussion involving a consideration of all these points, see MacIver, *The Web of Government*, pp. 147–174. It is interesting to note that Professor MacIver, in presenting his elaborate "conspectus of the forms of government" in which all of these factors are taken into account, found it "necessary to observe that in the endless processes of political change any form of government, as it exists at a particular moment, is likely to exhibit features characteristic of different types, while it is moving in one direction or another. This caution is obviously necessary when we are dealing with the economic basis (column B), but it is applicable everywhere." *Ibid.,* p. 150.

Although it is commonly believed that all dictatorships are basically alike, this is not the case. Each of the authoritarian regimes in operation in Europe before and since the war have certain characteristics indigenous to their respective countries; and hence little generalization is possible from one country to another.[5] Attempts have been made to secure a classification on the basis of structure, but such efforts have on the whole been unsuccessful. For example, Communist Russia and Nazi Germany were similar from the point of view of political structure; yet they differed fundamentally in their ultimate aims and philosophies. Although Fascist Italy had and Portugal has a "corporative" form of government; yet most observers agree that the spirit and temper of these two regimes were decidedly different.[6]

It is possible to use ideology as the basis for classification; but this method also involves difficulties. In Russia communist theory preceded and led to the regime. On the other hand, fascism evolved its philosophy after the march on Rome in order to rationalize what was being done and to give moral backing to certain measures that were being taken. However, in most other countries dictatorships have been more opportunistic so that psychological basis and philosophical doctrine have been less important.

The basis of the dictator's support varies considerably from country to country. It has sometimes been argued that peasants are more likely to submit to tyranny than industrial workers and that bolshevism and fascism are "unindustrial" because industrial organization is too complex to be directed by a dictatorship.[7] It is true that dictatorships have, for the most part, been confined to countries predominantly agricultural; but the exception, which dis-

5. It appears that the new regimes in the Soviet satellite countries constitute a divorce from their past and an almost complete acceptance of the Russian model. Whether the institutions in operation in these countries will in the course of time be modified in accordance with former habit and tradition remains to be seen.

6. For a comparison of the two, see Ernest Barker, *Reflections on Government* (London, 1942), pp. 341–366. See also Michael Derrick, *The Portugal of Salazar* (London, 1938); Herman Finer, *Mussolini's Italy* (New York, 1935).

7. Walter Lippmann, *A Preface to Morals* (New York, 1931), p. 253. "Dictatorship, based on a military hierarchy, administering the affairs of the community on behalf of the 'nation' or of the 'proletariat,' is nothing but a return to the natural organization of society in the pre-machine age. . . . Unable to master the industrial process by methods which are appropriate to it, the fascists and the bolshevists are attempting to master it by methods which antedate it."

proves the rule, was Nazi Germany.[8] Moreover, if absolutism is more common in backward agricultural states, it does not appear to be as firmly established nor to secure the degree of mass support as in the more modern industrial nations.[9]

Other writers have found a correlation between dictatorship and illiteracy.[10] Now it is undoubtedly true that democracy presumes an intelligent electorate and that the extent of illiteracy in Italy, Spain, Yugoslavia, Poland, Bulgaria, and Turkey is considerable. On the other hand, in few countries of the world are the cultural qualities of the average citizen greater than in Germany and Austria; and, as Professor Loewenstein has pointed out, if any reproach can be made to the inhabitants of these two countries, "it is that they have devoted themselves too much to political instruction and not too little." [11]

Although dictatorship has frequently been the refuge of groups associated with reaction, this is not always the case. In pre-war Hungary and Rumania the regime was maintained by a small oligarchy which sought to protect its privileged position. On the other hand, there are cases like that of Marshal Pilsudski who as dictator of Poland was generally opposed by parties of the right. Moreover, dictatorship has frequently brought a sharp break with the past and ushered in a social revolution. This was the declared aim of the Communist dictatorship of Russia as well as of Kemal Ataturk in Turkey. In other words, an autocratic regime may be radical, reactionary, liberal, or conservative. It may be, as in Yugoslavia when King Alexander resumed power in 1929, merely an honest effort to prevent disorder and to save the state.[12] Dictatorship has a long tradition, and it has come to all sorts of countries. Many different kinds of economic bases have furnished a support for dictatorships. Absolutism does not necessarily arise among "have not" nations nor among the vanquished.[13]

8. See Lindsay Rogers, *Crisis Government* (New York, 1934), pp. 39, 165. Professor Rogers appears to accept this thesis and argues that in Germany "fascism is emotional, not economic."

9. Diana Spearman, *Modern Dictatorship* (New York, 1939), p. 65.

10. See, for example, Francisco Cambo, *Les dictatures* (Paris, 1930).

11. "Autocracy versus Democracy," *op. cit.*, p. 586.

12. See Carlo Sforza, *European Dictatorships* (New York, 1931), pp. 100–118.

13. "A striking commentary on the variety of environments in which this phenomenon [dictatorship] flourishes is the fact that of the countries we here

20   *Why Democracies Fail*

The classification presented here is not exhaustive, and it will not furnish a method for classifying all authoritarian regimes.[14] It is instead an attempt to classify dictatorships that were in operation in Europe before the outbreak of war in 1939. It may be that it does not quite do that; for certain countries have features common to perhaps two or three of the principal types discussed here. However, this is inevitable; for, as Professor R. M. MacIver has pointed out, "No specific form of government endures, though there are certain major type-forms that have at least a relative permanence. Here is one reason why political structures are hard to classify. They are not like the genera and species of nature, which to a large extent persist and reproduce themselves even though new forms evolve." [15] In any case, the purpose of classification ought not to be merely an attempt to categorize facts but an attempt to establish some kind of relationship. The method used here is preferable to others in that it emphasizes more clearly fundamental differences in the character of modern dictatorships.[16]

---

review Italy was a victorious great power, Spain a war neutral, Russia an Entente great power that deserted to embark on a world crusade, Hungary a beaten minor power, Greece a neutral forced into half-hearted participation on both sides, and Poland a constant battle ground, participating on all three sides, Entente, Central, and Russian." Henry R. Spencer, "European Dictatorships," *The American Political Science Review*, XXI (1927), 539.

14. Professor Hermann Kantorowicz, *Dictatorships* (Cambridge, England: 1935), pp. 10–11, says: "But it ought, perhaps, to be pointed out that classifications, like definitions, are neither true nor false, but can be more or less useful, and that, as a rule, several classifications, although each must comply with certain well-known logical requirements, are equally possible, though not equally useful for the needs of a particular science. It would be tempting to classify dictatorships according to their ideologies, or to their economic programmes. But the immense literature on dictatorships has shown that this attempt would be premature: a great part of it is mere philosophic drawing-room talk or political propaganda. It has not even produced a handy terminology, still less a set of clear concepts, or a comprehensive classification. There are many writings allegedly on 'dictatorship' which are not aware that they are only thinking of the fascist type. There are still more writings explaining dictatorships as an expression of the interests of the 'capitalists,' or 'the lower middle classes,' or considering them as 'post-war phenomena,' or—especially Hitlerism—as consequences of a 'humiliating peace.' If these authors had taken the trouble first to define and then to classify the objects of their studies, they would have easily found that dictatorships, like monarchies or republics, can be filled with almost any contents, no matter whether socialist, capitalist, or precapitalist. . . . Without classification, concepts and terminology, no scientific description or comparison is feasible, and no psychological analysis, no historical research, however deep, however learned, can replace them."

15. *The Web of Government*, p. 147.

16. For a different classification of European dictatorships, see Diana Spearman, *Modern Dictatorship* (New York, 1939), pp. 15–16; Hermann Kantorowicz, "Dictatorships," *Politica*, I (August, 1935), 470–488.

ROYAL DICTATORSHIP

Sometimes prevailing institutions may not be functioning properly and the necessity may be felt for the king to resume power. In a case of this kind the pattern is similar to Tudor or Hohenzollern absolutism; for the dictatorship is based upon tradition and does not represent a sharp break with the past.[17] Although organized under a personal ruler, a dictatorship of this kind differs from fascism in that the king had a special claim to the allegiance of the whole country before he seized the government. Moreover, a royal dictatorship does not generally alter the underlying social structure but is merely an attempt to deal with a crisis of some kind.

The king may personally resume power or entrust it to a minister. For example, King Alexander of Yugoslavia established a personal dictatorship in 1929 after the country had experienced a complete breakdown of democratic government. Between 1918 and 1928 there had been twenty-three governments. After ten years of independence the different parts of the country were still living under the laws of their previous nationalities because no government had been in office long enough to produce a scheme for codification of the laws. After a Serbian deputy murdered the leader of the Croat Peasant party in the Assembly, the king found it impossible to find anyone who could form a government; and for three months Yugoslavia was without a government at all. Finally, the king resolved the problem by declaring himself dictator and disbanding the existing parties.

For similar reasons, King Boris III of Bulgaria [18] in 1935 and

17. Under monarchy succession to authority is stabilized whereas under a dictatorship it is not; and hence it may appear to be a contradiction in terms to speak of "royal dictatorship." On the other hand, dictatorship suggests the exercise of authority beyond or outside of what is considered normal in a constitutional regime. The word "tyrant" is sometimes used to suggest unmitigated personal authority; and on this basis either a king or a dictator, who ruled without respect for the law and for the rights of his subjects, could be considered a tyrant. See R. W. K. Hinton, "Was Charles I a Tyrant?" *The Review of Politics,* XVIII (January, 1956), 69–87. In the text "royal dictatorship" is used to convey the idea that absolutism has been established after an unsuccessful experiment with democracy. Although the Tudors and the Hohenzollerns were not "dictators," the authoritarian regimes which they established were probably not much different from the contemporary royal dictatorship.

18. "With feelings running so high, a durable working agreement among the parties was out of the question. In fact the party system had degenerated into more than fifteen warring groups. Their undignified scramble for the spoils of office undermined the prestige of government and caused much superfluous ex-

King Carol II of Rumania [19] in 1938 took personal charge of the government. In both Yugoslavia and Bulgaria there appears to have been considerable enthusiasm for the king's resumption of power, but in Rumania popular support for King Carol's dictatorship was at least problematical.[20]

Instead of exercising power himself, the king may turn his authority over to a minister, as King Alfonso XIII of Spain did to Primo de Rivera. Another illustration may be found in King George II of Greece who in 1936 handed authority over to General John Metaxas. In all of these cases the spirit of the government was quite different from fascism; and to call these governments "fascist" takes all meaning from the word.

MILITARY DICTATORSHIP

In many states the army is active in politics, and its officers, who are united into a closed group or caste, exercise an important influence in the councils of government. Under such circumstances control of the army often means control of the state, and the regular formula for a change of governments is the seizure of power by a general who has mustered sufficient support from his fellow officers. Under royal dictatorship the king and the military often work closely together; and many of the most important offices are held by army leaders.

The army may be used to push over a decadent government or to break a stalemate. For example, Turkey's "miracle man," Mustafa Kemal Pasha, liberated the country of foreign troops and gave a new lease on life to the "sick man of Europe." At the end of World War I Turkey was in a state of complete collapse. The old autocracy, based on religion, was inefficient and corrupt; and its military defeat appeared to be complete. For many years the

penditure—aside from corruption. Of Bulgaria's 96 ministers from the liberation up to 1926, no less than 48 were convicted by state tribunals; eight special courts were instituted to inquire into dishonest acts of cabinet members." Joseph S. Roucek, *The Politics of the Balkans* (New York, 1939), pp. 126–127.

19. "Carol's assumption of dictatorship is little to the liking of us who believe in democracy. But a politically backward country like Rumania, seething with discontent and torn by factional strife, is far from easy to rule; and it is probable that the King sincerely believes that a royal dictatorship offers the most practical solution of the difficult problem of government." Jonathan F. Scott, *Twilight of the Kings* (New York, 1938), p. 79.

20. Henry L. Roberts, *Rumania: Political Problems of an Agrarian State* (New Haven, 1951), pp. 206–210.

Ottoman Empire, which included many nationalities, had been gradually undermined by the spread of European ideas. Before the war her European provinces had successfully revolted and became national states; and the Turkish Empire would have probably been destroyed before 1914 were it not for the support and protection given to the sultan by Britain and Germany.

It appeared as though Turkey's defeat in the war was the final blow. Constantinople was occupied by allied troops, and by the Treaty of Sèvres Turkey practically ceased to exist.[21] However, with only 2000 war-worn soldiers whom he was officially ordered by the sultan's government to demobilize, Kemal entered upon an apparently hopeless conflict with the great powers—and won. His smashing defeat of the Greeks led to the scrapping of the dictate of Sèvres and to the Treaty of Lausanne, which was negotiated on equal terms between Turkey and the great powers. Turkey was invited to join the League of Nations, from which Germany was still excluded; and the new Turkey, recognized in this treaty, although smaller than before, enjoyed a high degree of ethnic homogeneity and, except for demilitarization and international supervision of the Straits, secured complete sovereign independence from foreign restrictions.

By any standard Kemal's accomplishments represented a remarkable combination of military and diplomatic skill; and to the majority of the Turks, who knew nothing of Anglo-French discords and Bolshevist dangers, it was nothing short of a miracle. It is easy to understand why it was that "when Kemal assumed power, the majority of the people certainly did not know what his policy was and probably felt little inclination to ask." [22]

The position of Marshal Josef Pilsudski in Poland was similar to that of Kemal in Turkey. He also was a war hero and had played a leading role in re-establishing the Polish state. Between 1772 and 1795 Poland was partitioned among Russia, Austria, and Prussia; and, except for a partial brief restoration during the

21. The Greek frontier was advanced to within a few miles of Constantinople; Turkey lost her rights in Smyrna and its hinterland to Greece; and on her Eastern frontier an Armenian republic was set up. Kurdistan was declared autonomous and the rest of Asia Minor was divided into spheres of influence and awarded to England, France, and Italy.

22. Spearman, *op. cit.*, p. 35. See also Thomas F. Ford, "Kamalist Turkey," in Guy Stanton Ford (ed.), *Dictatorship in the Modern World* (Minneapolis, 1939), pp. 126–153.

Napoleonic period as the Duchy of Warsaw, she disappeared for 125 years from the map of Europe. It was only in 1918 with Germany defeated, Austria-Hungary shattered, and Tsarist Russia dissolved in revolution, that the restoration of Poland became a possibility.

Although Polish nationalism remained alive during this period, the division tended to produce political groups, each with particular objectives and points of view, that continued after the restoration. Moreover, the people became hostile to government while under foreign rule and tended to carry over into the republic habits of conspiracy and intrigue they had developed in resisting their oppressors. In addition, Poland had within its borders a number of minority groups—White Russians, Lithuanians, Ruthenians, Germans, and Jews; for less than three-fourths of the population was of Polish nationality. All of these factors, not to mention lack of political experience, the high percentage of illiteracy, the poverty of the peasants, and factionalism within each party, tended to complicate Polish politics.

The result was that the Polish parliament (Sejm) consisted of about thirty passionate, disparate groups, each struggling for immediate advantages. Deputies spent most of their time in mutual recriminations, in the overthrow of ministries, and in the prolonged negotiations which preceded the formation of new coalitions. By May, 1926, there had been sixteen ministries; and hence no government was ever in office long enough to deal with the financial crisis or give any practical results. Useful bills were frequently rejected by the legislature, not on their merits, but as the result of factious opposition. In other words, the country was faced with perpetual deadlock, and it was not without some justification that Pilsudski charged that the Sejm was hated and despised throughout the country.

In May, 1926, Pilsudski marched on Warsaw with three regiments; and after three days of street fighting forced President Wojciechowski and Prime Minister Witos to resign. After the *coup d'état* Pilsudski declined the office of prime minister but agreed to serve as Minister of War in the newly appointed Bartel cabinet. Later he declined to serve as President but did accept the post of prime minister. However, regardless of the office he held, Pilsudksi was the real power in Poland and his influence remained unimpaired until his death in 1935. Although Pilsudski dominated the political life of the country and although the effective government was a military dictatorship,[23] a certain freedom of opinion remained in that the Parliament was not abolished and opposition parties were permitted to exist, even though their activities were drastically curtailed.[24]

The regime of Generalissimo Francisco Franco of Spain stands in a category by itself. Although General Franco has used many of the ideas, trappings, and devices of European fascism, he is also a product of Spanish history and must be thought of as "Spain's latest in a long line of Primo de Riveras." [25] Moreover, the fascist party of Spain, the Falange, is only one of the forces supporting the regime and at the present time is not even the dominant one. The *"caudillo"* is kept in power by a coalition of forces—among which are the army, business and financial interests, and the Roman Catholic Church—who are able to subdue their differences in order to support the regime. Apart from the Falange, which is an innovation, the elements supporting the Franco dictatorship are roughly the same as those which have been the bulk of every Spanish government in modern times except, of course, the one overthrown in the Spanish civil war.

The force of tradition, as well as an attempt to appease the monarchists, may be seen in the recent decree declaring Spain to be a kingdom, without a king, but with a "Regency Council" under Franco's direction which has authority to choose a royal successor providing that the person chosen is thirty years of age and swears to uphold the existing regime. The discordant elements

23. Pilsudski is reported to have said in 1926: "Within the reborn nation there was no rebirth of the people's soul, save in the army." Sigmund Neumann, *Permanent Revolution* (New York, 1942), p. 70.

24. "Pilsudski's *coup d'état* was inspired less by personal ambition than by a belief that Poland was drifting back to the anarchy that had preceded the Partitions. . . . His régime probably prevented the growth of anarchy, which might have invited foreign intervention, and ended the 'mania of conspiracy' which had plagued Poland in the past; it improved public administration and finance; furthered the unification of the three divisions of the country; greatly strengthened the army; and made peace with Germany. In tolerating the existence of Parliament after the *coup d'état* of 1926 and in consenting to long delays in the formulation of a new constitution, Pilsudski displayed a patience lacking in authoritarian chiefs of other states. He unified various factions without undermining traditional Polish values and without completely destroying liberty." Raymond Leslie Buell, *Poland: Key to Europe* (Second edition; New York, 1939), pp. 89, 95.

25. S. Grover Rich, Jr., "Franco Spain: A Reappraisal," *Political Science Quarterly*, LXVII (September, 1952), 380.

behind General Franco are held together because the only alternative appears to be a continuation of the ruinous civil war. However, the regime has many opponents not only among its defeated republican enemies but also among powerful monarchist groups as well.

The task confronting General Franco is to steer a course which maintains the support of those behind his regime. The fact that he must take into account these various groups limits his power and forces him to pursue a course of some moderation. Although the Franco regime has certain fascist features, the fundamental character of Spanish society has remained largely the same, and there has been no "fascist revolution." The main prop behind the Spanish dictatorship is still the army together with the classes and interests which the army represents. It is generally agreed that Franco, like many of his predecessors, will remain in power so long as he can continue to secure support from "the generals." [26]

Military dictators are not always reactionary, as is sometimes supposed; and they frequently do a great deal of good. The Turkish Republic was created out of war by military men; to a limited degree Kemal always relied upon the army to maintain his power; yet his regime was dedicated to bringing about a radical social transformation in the country and its avowed aim was to prepare Turkey ultimately for democracy.[27] Marshal Pilsudski, stern old man that he was, championed the interests of peasants and was generally opposed by the parties of the right. When an army general gets into politics, he tends to make the state into an army. This means that he is generally unwilling to tolerate the untidiness of civil life, that he will assign functions in terms of hierarchical grades, and that he will put an emphasis on unity. Under certain circumstances a military dictator may do a great deal of good. For example, Marshal Pilsudski was able, temporarily at least, to

26. "It should be made clear that any internal overthrow of the Franco régime will depend ultimately for its success upon the Army. . . . Only the Army can qualify, and a successful *coup d'état,* supported by disgruntled business men and monarchist landowners, is probably the way Franco will finally meet his downfall." S. Grover Rich, Jr., *op. cit.,* p. 383.

27. For a long time Turkey had one-party government, but in the late 1930's an official opposition was permitted in the National Assembly although its size was limited to sixteen members. However, in the 1950 elections the Republican People's party, the governing party, was defeated; and to everyone's surprise the opposition, the Democratic party, took office.

restore order, break the deadlock, and supply a greater efficiency in administration.

THE PARTY DICTATORSHIP

It was in Russia that the world first witnessed the triumph of a single political party which enjoys a monopoly of political power, regards itself as an élite, requires a period of probation for applicants for membership, and deliberately keeps its membership restricted. This concept of a self-dedicated élite is not found in Marx, and in many ways it is contrary to the whole idea of a proletarian revolution. However, Lenin saw that a mass of illiterates with little political consciousness could not bring about a revolution.[28] Therefore, the proletariat must be guided by "its most advanced part, the Communist party," which has in its membership a core of men who are tested by experience, undeviating in discipline, and wholehearted in their devotion to the cause.

According to Article 126 of the Soviet Constitution the Communist party is to act as "the vanguard of the working people in their struggle to strengthen and develop the socialist system." This means that members of the party are supposed to serve as an inspiration, example, and educator of the masses; that their conduct is supposed to win admiration and respect for the party; and that in both legislation and administration the party controls at all times. Members of the party not only direct and control the work of the Soviet and other governmental organs but they are also supposed to see that all mass organizations, such as trade unions, co-operatives, youth organizations, and cultural organizations, accept the party's leadership and carry out its instructions. The Soviet Constitution frankly states that the party is "the leading core of all organizations of the working people, both public and state," and Joseph Stalin has written that "no important political or organizational problem is ever decided by our soviets and other mass organizations without directives from the Party. . . . the dicta-

28. Lenin is reported to have said in a speech before the second congress of the Communist International: ". . . in the era of capitalism, when the masses of the workers are constantly subjected to exploitation and cannot develop their human faculties, the most characteristic feature of working class political parties is that they can embrace only a minority of their class. . . . That is why we must admit that only this class-conscious minority can guide the broad masses of the workers and lead them." See Hans Kelsen, *The Political Theory of Bolshevism* (Berkeley, 1949), p. 52.

torship of the proletariat is, *substantially,* the 'dictatorship' of its vanguard, the 'dictatorship' of its Party, as the force which guides the proletariat." [29]

Rank and file members of the Communist party exert little influence on major policy decisions. Decision-making is concentrated in a small and virtually permanent group of party officials, and higher organs of the party dictate to those beneath them. A party member has the duty to carry out all party instructions, and failure to conform to the "party line" has generally meant expulsion from the party. Even Lenin's assumption that there could be criticism of major ideas and policies within the party was replaced under Stalin by the notion of the infallibility of the leader. Thus party dogma governs all spheres of Soviet life and dominates the citizen's cultural and social as well as his political life.

Although communism and fascism have different political philosophies, their pattern of political and social organization was very much the same. In Nazi Germany and Fascist Italy, as well as in Communist Russia, a single party, which was autocratically organized and intolerant of opposition, had a monopoly of political power. In all three countries the party was totalitarian in the sense that it sought to bring all cultural and spiritual, as well as political and economic, aspects of national life into harmony with and under control of the regime. Party organization stood along side of or parallel to that of the government so that the same persons exercised both party and state functions; but the most important common characteristic of all three parties is that they were a compact and integrated group, set off sharply from the general mass of citizens and purposely kept small enough to enable exacting standards to be maintained and rigid discipline to be enforced. In other words, the party was supposed to embrace the élite of the nation and constituted an inner group in contrast to the masses outside.[30]

Inherent in this doctrine of the élite is the notion of superiority.

---

29. Joseph Stalin, *Leninism* (New York, 1928), I, 33.
30. There is much useful information in Waldemar Gurian, "The Rise of Totalitarianism in Europe," *Annual Report of the American Historical Association* (Washington: United States Government Printing Office, 1944), III, 297–304. See also by the same author, "The Sources of Hitler's Power," *The Review of Politics* (October, 1942), IV, 379–408, and M. A. Fitzsimons, "Die Deutschen Briefe: Gurian and the German Crisis," *The Review of Politics* (January, 1955), XVII, 47–72.

There is the inner group of certain select people who constitute the party and the great bulk of the masses who remain outside. The notion of superiority may be based upon dialectical ability, as in Russia, or it may be based upon blood, even if it is necessary to invent the blood. In any case, there is supposedly a body of truth to which the party has access and counter-ideologies cannot be tolerated.

Although government does not ordinarily create the social order that it sustains, party dictatorship tends to cut across pre-existing class lines and to set up a new type of social class identified with the party. In other words, there may be little connection between the social pyramid and the pyramid established by the idea of the élite. As a matter of fact, it may be that the party, as in Russia, is bent on destroying traditional class distinctions. In any case, the party hierarchy pulverizes in time the old social structure and sets up a new class system in which classes are distinguished by nearness or remoteness from seats of political power. In the Soviet Union traditional class distinctions have been abolished, but the leaders in public life and the heads of industry are drawn overwhelmingly from the Communist party. Since industrial executives and government administrators hold positions of power and with greater power goes greater prestige, greater opportunity, and greater privilege, it is easy to see that there is a new class system in which the party hierarchy is distinguished from those outside of the party and that, in general, those outside of the party enjoy a lower status.

DIFFERENCES IN PARTY DICTATORSHIPS

Although communism and fascism have a number of common characteristics and are similar in many ways, all party dictatorships are not alike. A distinction in the spirit and temper of certain of these regimes can be at least partially explained in terms of the purpose held by the party and the manner in which it came to power. For example, the party may be organized outside of the parliamentary system and have for its purpose the destruction of the existing institutional system. In the United States and Great Britain representative government was a going concern before political parties developed. Thus the party system was worked out within a given institutional setup and certain tacit assumptions were made by all major parties. However, in certain other countries political parties have grown up before or outside of the parliamentary system, and hence the party may not be devoted to the institutional system and may consider itself as a final authority. The Bolshevik party grew up in Russia when parliamentarism was non-existent and had as its aim or purpose the complete destruction of the existing social order. Although the Nazis had their origin after the Weimar Constitution was in operation, the party did not claim to be a reflection of public opinion but a "movement" apart from and above the parliamentary system.

A second set of circumstances which may produce a party dictatorship is when a number of parties try to operate the parliamentary system but are unable to do so because of the number of parties. Under these circumstances one party may seize power. Such a regime is similar to a military dictatorship; for although opposition parties are suppressed, the government does not as a rule try to wipe them out completely or change the existing social system.

Perhaps the best illustration is the dictatorship of Chancellor Engelbert Dollfuss in Austria. From the earliest days of the republic there existed a bitter feeling between the workers of Vienna, who had socialistic and anti-clerical leanings and who formed the core of the Social Democratic party, and the remaining Austrians, who were generally agrarian, conservative, religious, and bitterly anti-Marxian and who supported the Christian Socialist and Pan-German parties. The bitterness between Vienna and the rural hinterland expressed itself openly in the organization of two rival militant bodies: the agrarian Heimwehr and the socialist Schutzbund. The existence of these private armies did nothing to make the government's task easier. Considerable quantities of munitions and war supplies were stored away in secret hiding places; and there were frequent clashes between opposing groups. It has been estimated that the Schutzbund had in 1931 a trained membership of about ninety thousand men and that the Heimwehr included approximately sixty thousand armed men.[31] Since Austria's national army was limited by the peace treaty to thirty thousand men, the government really had the smallest armed force in the country.

31. Walter S. Langsam, *The World Since 1914* (Third edition; New York, 1936), p. 519.

On March 4, 1933, the National Council virtually adjourned itself indefinitely when the Speaker and both Deputy-Speakers resigned in the midst of an excited discussion on a bill to amnesty strikers on the government-owned railways. The bill was defeated by a vote of 81 to 80; but the presiding officer of the assembly, who was a Social Democrat and who had been unable to vote, resigned his office. His successor, the First Vice-President, was a Christian-Socialist, and hence on the next vote the opposition would have gained one vote and the government have lost one. He also resigned. The Second Vice-President, a Pan-German and a member of the opposition at this time, realized that with the removal of his vote the government would again have a majority of one; so he resigned. No provision of the constitution covered a situation of this kind with the result that Parliament became incapacitated. According to law, Parliament was unable legally to reconvene because only one of these three men could call a meeting; and all three had resigned their posts.

On March 7 Chancellor Dollfuss announced that although Parliament had become incapacitated the executive had not. President Miklas thereupon invested Dollfuss with emergency powers and the government ruled by decree.[32]

Another type of party dictatorship occurs when the party is synthetically created out of a pre-existing authoritarian system. The dictatorship finds that it cannot go on; and it thus becomes necessary to create a sort of ersatz party to carry on the regime. Perhaps the outstanding example was King Carol of Rumania. The king seized power but found that his royal dictatorship could not function as in the good old days. The result was that he tried to organize a popular party, the Front of National Rebirth, to support his dictatorship. This new single-party became the only recognized political organization in the state and membership in it was made obligatory for all officials.[33]

*   *   *   *   *   *

32. For a discussion of the events leading to the anti-Nazi dictatorship in Austria, see Stephen Raushenbush, *The March of Dictatorship* (New Haven, 1939), pp. 284–313; Langsam, *op. cit.*, pp. 510–535.

33. C. Kormos, *Rumania* (Cambridge, 1944), p. 85; Roberts, *op. cit.*, p. 208. As is well known, Carol's efforts, although temporarily successful, ended in disaster. Although the Iron Guard was outlawed and its leaders were arrested, he was not able to destroy its influence. This was partially because of the support it enjoyed outside of Rumania in Germany and Italy.

Although the power of the dictator is the central fact in any form of absolutism, this power derives its meaning from the scheme of society and the view of life represented by the regime, the process of building it, and the consequences that flow from it. The pattern of a military dictatorship is different from that of a fascist one-party state; and just as Cromwell's dictatorship was different from the absolute monarchy of Charles I, so the motivations and loyalty structure of military dictatorships are different from those of a royal dictatorship.

Although foreign influence is frequently in evidence, authoritarian regimes all have the distinctive characteristics of their respective countries. The ruthless extermination of all those who endanger the security of the regime is a cardinal feature of any form of absolutism, but the demand for monopoly control may vary considerably from country to country. For example, there is a great deal of difference between the ruthless suppression of opponents under the Nazi, Fascist, or Soviet dictatorships and the Austrian or Portuguese regimes in which opposition always existed in the shadow and the rule was more bearable because it was not nearly so arbitrary.

Chapter 4 ⎯⎯⎯⎯⎯⎯⎯⎯⎯⎯⎯⎯⎯

EMPIRICAL CAUSES

OF DICTATORSHIP

THERE is perhaps no single set of causes for dictatorship. In modern Europe absolutism has appeared in very different countries, under different circumstances, and for very different reasons. Although in each country it was imposed to deal with a crisis of some kind, there was no similarity in social structure, economic organization, national tradition, or race.[1] Although the historical background and social conditions were very different, it was this general background which helped determine the type of dictatorship which emerged. Although the discussion in this chapter is general and applicable to any type of constitutional democracy, it is concerned primarily with parliamentary systems. This is because the presidential system, with the exception of the ill-fated French constitution of 1848, has been avoided on the continent of Europe on the theory that so powerful an executive might easily become dictatorial.[2]

1. "Germany, Nordic, industrial, and largely Protestant, succumbed as easily as Poland, chiefly agricultural, Slav and Catholic. Italy, with a strongly Liberal tradition, accepted an autocrat as quickly as Turkey, which had never known any other form of government. Nor can a common factor be found in the crisis which preceded dictatorship. The difficulties which led to dictatorship arose from the most varied causes." Spearman, *op. cit.*, pp. 77–78.

2. For a discussion of this point, see Karl Loewenstein, "The Presidency Outside of the United States," *The Journal of Politics*, XI (1949), 447–496. Henry Hazlitt, *A New Constitution Now* (New York, 1942), p. 17, attributes a

EXECUTIVE IMPOTENCE

Perhaps the greatest operational weakness of popular government has been its inability to provide effective political leadership within the traditional institutional framework. In the eighteenth and nineteenth centuries there was a reaction against executives, and during this period legislatures everywhere gained in power. The struggle was first an attempt to establish parliaments as a counterpoise to the Crown and then, as election came to be looked upon as the primary basis of authority, to dominate the executive and bring the specialized bureaucracy under parliamentary control. Thus the memory of an old regime of executive absolutism caused the assembly to be jealous of its power and to be constantly on the alert against the new executive in order to prevent its reversion to the old type.

Today there is a reaction against weak executive power because social and economic conditions are of such a nature as to demand swift and drastic executive action. Perhaps one of the most dramatic cleavages between constitutional intent and political reality has been that legislative supremacy has so frequently led to the establishment of dictatorship. This is because government requires the concentration of political power in a small compact group. A multi-membered assembly, torn by party dissensions and subject to the fluctuating moods of public opinion, is incapable of governing. The most such an assembly can do is control the government it places in the chair of authority. It is an interesting fact that in no European country has the aggrandizement of a strong constitutional executive led towards authoritarian rule. It is instead a weak executive, incapable of providing effective govern-

---

good deal of the blame for the rise of dictatorship in Latin America to an independent executive modelled upon the American President, but his analysis is based upon a misconception of both the presidential and parliamentary systems as they operate in their mother countries. For a discussion see Norman L. Stamps, "The American Presidential System," *Political Quarterly*, XXV (April–June, 1954), 155–165; and "A Reappraisal of American Political Institutions," *The Southwestern Social Science Quarterly*, XXIV (December, 1953), 47–59. It is, of course, true that presidential government has not achieved notable success south of the Rio Grande; but its failure in these countries has been more because it has not had a fair trial than because of a particular organization of the executive branch. See Russell H. Fitzgibbon, "Pathology of Democracy in Latin America, A Political Scientist's Point of View," *American Political Science Review*, XLIV (March, 1950), 118–129.

ment, that has been replaced by a strong executive free from legislative control.

In Italy the country was faced with serious economic difficulties. There was mounting unemployment, economic dislocation brought about by the war, a seething discontent not only on the part of workers but also of veterans who returned home to find that they had no jobs and that the sacrifices they had made benefited the profiteers. The socialists, who had opposed the war, benefited from the general disappointment felt in the peace treaties and Italy's failure to secure the colonial territories she had expected. Although the cost of living was still rising, employers sought to reduce wages on the theory that labor costs had increased during the war far beyond their real value. The government apparently, because of successive splits in the party system, was unable to agree upon a consistent policy of any kind. In the meantime, a wave of strikes swept over Italy leading towards even further dislocations in the economy. Finally, the workers in many places sought to take over forcibly the property of their employers and run the factories themselves; but the government did nothing to protect legal rights or restore order. It is probably true, as has frequently been pointed out, that the workers could not operate the plants and that the government's policy of letting the storm "blow itself out" could only end in the failure of the workers to accomplish their objectives. Nevertheless, many employers were permanently alienated by the government's inaction; and it is undoubtedly true that the government's failure to restore law and order, enforce legal guarantees, and develop a policy to meet with the economic crisis meant the loss of respect and prestige among other groups as well. As the situation degenerated still further into a kind of civil war between fascist bands and socialist groups, the government still could not think of anything constructive. Sometimes it was glad that Mussolini's supporters had broken a troublesome strike; at other times perhaps those in the governing coalition hoped to benefit politically by the forcible "retirement" of socialist mayors and other officials in the provinces. In any case, the country experienced a period of lawlessness in which there were beatings and murders on both sides and duly elected officials, mostly socialist mayors, were forced to retire from office. Although there was chaos and an obvious need for drastic action, the government did nothing.

An atmosphere had thus been created which was most beneficial to extremist groups; and it was at this time that people flocked to join the Fascist party. As Professor Gaetano Salvemini has said,

> While the forces which were to destroy democratic institutions in Italy were being massed and organized, the Chamber of Deputies was discrediting itself with inconclusive battles of words and trivial acts of violence. It finally reached a point where it was unable to create a cabinet that was worthy of anything but contempt.
>
> Decidedly, a disease was undermining the Italian political constitution—a parliamentary paralysis. And outside Parliament there was another disease at work—civil war. Either Parliament must recover its powers and put an end to the civil war, or parliamentary institutions would break down in Italy.[3]

Although Mussolini had only thirty-five deputies in the Chamber, he finally challenged the government itself. It was only then that the cabinet decided to take action, but it was too late. The king, upon being advised that the Fascists had infiltrated the army and the police, refused to permit the government to declare martial law, accepted the cabinet's resignation, and asked Mussolini to become premier.[4]

PARTY STALEMATE

The major cause of executive impotence has been party deadlock in the legislature. Since parliamentary government makes the executive dependent upon and responsible to a majority in the representative assembly, all governmental activity becomes paralyzed if the assembly becomes divided into so many factions that there cannot be found a stable majority for the executive's support. For example, there were twelve parties in the Italian Parliament before the Fascist revolution and fifteen in the German Reichstag in 1928. As this paralysis crept in, the people in country after country lost hope that effective action ever would be produced and "parliamentarism" became a by-word for inefficiency and inaction.

3. Lectures on Post-War Italy (mimeographed) delivered at Harvard University, quoted by Ferdinand A. Hermens, *Europe Between Democracy and Anarchy* (Notre Dame, 1951), p. 54.

4. For a discussion of events before the rise of Mussolini, see Henry R. Spencer, *Government and Politics of Italy* (Yonkers, 1932), pp. 11–114; Herbert W. Schneider, *Making the Fascist State* (New York, 1928); Herman Finer, *Mussolini's Italy* (New York, 1935); Gaetano Salvemini, *The Fascist Dictatorship in Italy* (New York, 1927).

This fact raises a number of fundamental issues concerning the party system and its functions in the governmental system. In the first place, what is the purpose of parties and what should be the subject of party controversy? Acting alone the individual citizen can do nothing, and it appears obvious that a principal aim of political parties is to organize the chaotic public will and educate the private citizen to political responsibility. However, not everything can be the subject of party controversy. By following obstructionist tactics a party can paralyze the work of an assembly and sabotage parliamentary institutions. Even though a minority and regularly defeated when votes are taken, such a party can delay debates and prevent the majority from bringing them to a conclusion, hurl insults, resort to disorderly conduct and a program of violence, and employ other techniques designed to prevent the normal operation of democratic institutions. Obviously a government must remove such obstacles; for it will otherwise be unable to act decisively and its opponents may profit from the chaos and confusion which they have caused; yet if the government goes too far in cutting off the fringes of dissent, it will have thereby destroyed the very principles upon which democracy is based. Democracy assumes that the minority will accept the rule of the majority and that the majority, in turn, will not rule too oppressively. In other words, both the majority and minority have rights but they also have obligations. It is the duty of the majority as represented in the government to govern and of the minority to confine its opposition to appeals to public opinion. Although the *raison d'être* of the opposition is to discuss and criticize and thereby educate public opinion, it does not have the right to follow obstructionist tactics.

There is also the question concerning how to correlate party responsibility with executive action. For example, the multiple party system in Germany was furthered by proportional representation so that there were regularly between ten and fifteen parties in the Reichstag. The result was that no government could command a majority in the legislature and that any combination of parties for the assumption of responsibility could always be defeated by a combination of those in opposition. Moreover, the electoral system discouraged a spirit of moderation and cooperation among the parties, not only because it gave representation to extremist groups, but also because each party was able to win seats on its own program without compromising its position and without taking into consideration the marginal voter. Although the power of dissolution was used five times prior to Hitler's appointment as Chancellor, it did not materially change the result; and President von Hindenburg was finally compelled to use Article 48 of the Weimar Constitution to make it possible for the government to function at all.

Although the President may be criticized because he permitted the use of Article 48 to chancellors whom he liked and refused it to others whom he disliked, the point is that the President was able to use his discretion because the party situation was such that it was impossible to form a government with majority support. Therefore, if von Hindenburg is to be criticized for the use of Article 48, rather than the manner of its use, the question arises as to what could he have done. There was no other way to get a budget enacted and to carry on the government. Professor Lindsay Rogers maintains that it was not resort to Article 48 which made for dictatorship in Germany. He points out that every government must be capable of meeting an emergency and that in both Great Britain and the United States the executive is able to act and deal with a crisis. Although the frequent resort to Article 48 created important precedents for Hitler and made his demands appear less revolutionary, Professor Rogers maintains that, given the circumstances present in Germany, the use of Article 48 proved to be an indispensable means of dealing with the emergency.[5]

Party stalemate also raises a question concerning the proper function of the legislature. A parliament is an admirable instrument for the expression of grievance and for the discussion of large principles. Its purpose is to discuss and guide the general conduct of the government, but it does not exist in order to govern. As a matter of fact, it may be argued that a legislative assembly is too numerous and too incoherent even to legislate directly and that it is bound by its nature to accept or reject proposals offered to it by the execu-

5. Lindsay Rogers et al., "Aspects of German Political Institutions," *Political Science Quarterly*, XLVII (1932), 321–351, 576–601. See also Frederick M. Watkins, *The Failure of Constitutional Emergency Powers under the German Republic* (Cambridge, 1939); H. J. Heneman, *The Growth of Executive Power in Germany: A Study of the German Presidency* (Minneapolis, 1934); Clinton Rossiter, *Constitutional Dictatorship* (Princeton, 1948), pp. 29–73.

tive power. This is the view set forth by John Stuart Mill in a famous passage of *Representative Government:*

> Instead of the function of governing, for which it is radically unfit, the proper office of a representative assembly is to watch and control the government: . . . to be at once the nation's Committee of Grievances and its Congress of Opinions. . . . Nothing but the restriction of the function of representative bodies within these rational limits, will enable the benefits of popular control to be enjoyed in conjunction with the no less important requisites (growing ever more important as human affairs increase in scale and complexity) of skilled legislation and administration.[6]

In any case, a legislative chamber composed of five or six hundred people of divergent political outlook cannot really govern; but it can prevent the government from doing so.

The successful operation of parliamentary government, therefore, requires a delicate balance between the legislature and the executive. In Great Britain cabinet government is characterized by a strong sense of unity. This is because the government generally has behind it a stable majority in Parliament. The cabinet links the executive branch of the government to the legislative; and in this capacity it leads the legislature and provides Parliament with the policy upon which decisions are made. Although cabinet proposals are criticized and vigorously opposed by the minority party, even the opposition expects to follow in most instances. Although the legislature is not a rubber-stamp, its proper role in Britain is generally confined to a review of the government's policies, discussion of these policies, the airing of grievances, and the reflection of public opinion.

There are many reasons why the government enjoys so much prestige, but the principal reason is that the cabinet constitutes the leaders of the majority party and is representative in its membership of the party. Moreover, the majority party received a popular mandate at the last election. The system is unusually sensitive to public opinion because there is a two-party system and because the two parties are supported by almost an equal number of voters. Hence only the slightest shift in popular support will change the minority into a majority. The government, therefore, must constantly keep

6. *Representative Government* (Everyman's Library; New York, 1936) pp. 239–241.

its ear to the ground and carry out its policies in accordance with public opinion; yet the cabinet exercises control over the House of Commons through the threat of dissolution, strict party discipline, and the introduction of all legislative proposals.

On the Continent of Europe a satisfactory equilibrium between legislative and executive power has not been achieved. In England Parliament was eventually bypassed, and the cabinet came to possess a kind of plebiscitary authority derived from the people themselves. However, in France and in European states generally this relationship did not develop because of a failure to polarize the people's partisan allegiances as in England, and hence Continental parliaments became tribunals for making and unmaking ministries. Such a system also conforms to the belief, derived from the French Revolution, that political power is a delegation from the individual citizen through the legislature to an executive dependent on that legislature. Such a view is also rooted in European experience. Having evolved in opposition to absolute monarchy, European constitutionalism has been haunted by fear of a strong executive. However, parliamentary omnipotence, by its inherent functional defects, has provoked a swing of the pendulum back to the extreme of executive ascendancy; and whenever a nation re-emerged from dictatorship, it almost automatically reverted to the supremacy of the legislature. Thus European constitutional history since the French Revolution, as Professor Karl Loewenstein has pointed out, "may be visualized as the perennial quest for a formula for what should be the proper relationship between executive and legislative powers." [7]

The historical experience with assembly government shows quite clearly that it is ill-adapted to conditions in the modern world. It is a system with checks but without balance, and it has proved itself unable to cope with the growing need for more governmental action and more definite leadership. Since assembly government prevents the concentration of power in a small committee which is characteristic of modern cabinet government, the executive is incapable of performing the long-range policy and

7. "The Presidency Outside the United States," *The Journal of Politics,* XI (1949), 462. See also by the same author, "The Balance Between Legislative and Executive Power: A Study in Comparative Constitutional Law," *The University of Chicago Law Review,* V (1938), 566–608.

planning functions which are now required of modern governments. The result is that assembly government, whenever it has been faced by an exceptional crisis, has been compelled to resort to dictatorial "emergency" powers. In other words, the principal defect of this system has been its inability to find a satisfactory means whereby governmental leadership through action can be subordinated to the political control by parliament. Generally speaking, it may be said that the people have been compelled to choose between an executive free from political control but able to secure swift and drastic action and an executive subject to political control but unable to pursue a coherent and consistent policy. The history of parliamentarism on the Continent of Europe seems to affirm that government by an elected assembly or subject to direct dictation and interference by such an assembly cannot work. In any case, as Professor Karl Loewenstein has pointed out, assembly government has frequently been the façade behind which a strong executive and eventually authoritarianism and dictatorship established themselves. "There is no other form of constitutional government which lends itself so readily to the domination of the state by a strong personality, or group, faction or party." [8]

Lack of Agreement on Fundamental Matters

Democracy is a delicate form of government which rests upon conditions which are rather precarious. For representative institutions to function successfully there must be a wide area of agreement on fundamental matters and a willingness to compromise on others. The great advantage which the British government had during the nineteenth century was that the differences which divided the two parties were on methods of action rather than on deep-seated principles. The Whigs and Tories, Liberals and Conservatives were united in their desire to preserve the monarchy, the established Church, and the main tenets of the economic system.

> After the triumph of free trade, there was hardly a measure carried to the statute-book by one government which could not equally have been put there by its rivals. If the Liberals carried free trade, the Tories gave the trade unions their charter of emancipation. If the Liberals were responsible for the Reform Act of 1832, the Tories carried that of 1867; and 1884 was a compromise between them. Each shares in the credit for

8. *Ibid.*, p. 476.

the reform of local government. Each laid a great foundation-stone in the structure of national education. Neither in foreign nor in imperial policy would it be easy to find differences between them of a thorough-going character; even over Ireland the distinction between them, as the ultimate solution made clear, was one of degree rather than of kind.[9]

In other words, the two parties were in agreement as to the kind of state they wanted, and there was little difference in their social composition. Being in agreement on the broad and general principles which ought to guide the policies of government, they could proceed to disagree on the best means of achieving the aims or goals they both had in common. There were, of course, differences of opinion, but they were concerned primarily with matters of degree and emphasis rather than with the fundamental structure of society or the form of government. Under such circumstances government by discussion and majority vote works best because compromise is possible at all pivotal points and because the minority can meet defeat at the polls in good temper since it need not regard the decision as either a fatal or a permanent surrender of its vital interests.

It is impossible to overestimate the extent to which the success of parliamentary government is dependent upon a considerable measure of agreement on fundamentals. The device of alternating government and opposition is possible only because the minority consents to lose and is willing to accept the rule of the majority. The opposition party is willing to do this because it can, when it comes to office again, take up the threads of its activity more or less where it left them. It is prepared to accept the risks of the next

9. Harold J. Laski, *Democracy in Crisis* (Chapel Hill, 1933), pp. 33–34. Although Laski's main emphasis was on social classes, Professor Ferdinand A. Hermens has pointed out that the empirical character of British and American politics can be explained by the existence of a two-party system which has been maintained by the electoral system. The single-member district with plurality election has a profound effect upon the psychology of politics because it encourages the voter to identify himself with a broadly based political movement so as not to "waste" his vote and because it compels political parties to modify their programs and make a broad appeal in order to attract the marginal voter. On the other hand, proportional representation has a disintegrating effect upon society because it increases the number of political parties and because it encourages a programmatic dogmatism by making it possible for candidates to win seats without taking other views into account. See his *Democracy or Anarchy? A Study of Proportional Representation* (Notre Dame, 1941) and *Europe Between Democracy and Anarchy* (Notre Dame, 1951); Maurice Duverger, *Political Parties* (New York, 1954), pp. 206–228 and 245–255.

election because it knows that in the meantime the fundamental contours of the state will remain unchanged and that eventually it is certain of office again.

When differences of opinion within a state become irreconcilable and passionate and when individuals or groups refuse peaceably to lose, constitutional government breaks down. For example, in Portugal a substantial portion of the people refused to accept the republic and wanted a monarchy. Under such circumstances it was impossible for the republican system to operate because the government was compelled, in order to maintain the regime, to cut off the fringes of dissent and thus itself became authoritarian. Under such circumstances the dominant interest in the state establishes control by force and governs by coercion rather than by consent.[10] Only a firmly established government is capable of being constitutionalized.

Every one of the dictatorships was characterized by a basic disagreement of this kind, but perhaps the situation in Spain furnishes the best example. In the election held in November, 1933, there were about eighteen political parties which were equally divided with six on the right, six in the center, and six on the left. The right wanted a monarchical Catholic regime, but they were not united. Some wanted the old king; some a regent; others favored a different royal house; and still others who were agreed on property and religion wanted the state headed by a different sort of ruler. When the civil war came, these groups tended to fuse, and out of this combination came still a different type of movement.

On the left were the syndicalists, who stood for the destruction of the state and the reconstruction of society on the basis of autonomous syndicates; the anarchists, who tended to fuse with the syndicalists; the communists, who loathed these groups but who were themselves split into Stalinists and Trotskyites; and the socialists, who were split into a number of factions. The center

10. One of the techniques used by most dictators is to distinguish between the "real" and the empiric. There is an underlying something which is the real country and which the party will bring forth. Thus the "real" Portugal is altogether different from the existing Portugal. Both the Russian and the German, as well as most other, dictatorships have used this device. For example, Lenin said that the peasants are ignorant and probably would rush back into private property, but the "real" Russia is crying to be communized.

was very weak, for Spain had practically no middle class; and it was finally crushed in the war.

There was, therefore, no agreement as to what the state should be; and the differences which separated these many groups were of such a fundamental nature as to be practically irreconcilable by compromise and persuasion. As a matter of fact, this picture of eighteen political parties makes the situation in Spain appear more simple than it actually was; for there were also the issue of federalism and the clerical question which tended to cut diagonally across all party lines. Thus the Basques, often referred to as the most Catholic of all the Spanish, fought with the loyalists and held out against Franco to the end, not because they agreed with the anticlerical policies of the government, but because they favored autonomy for their area and believed that this could best be secured from the loyalist regime.[11]

The breakdown of democracy in Yugoslavia furnishes another illustration of how a bitter cleavage over fundamental principles can sabotage a parliamentary system. Here there were differences of opinion concerning social and economic policies as elsewhere, but the factors dividing the nation into two irreconcilable parts were mainly geographical and cultural. Although the Serbs and Croats belong to the same race and speak the same language, their history and traditions are different. For centuries Serbia formed a part of the Turkish Empire, while Croatia was a part of the Austrian Empire. Hence the Serbs were Greek Orthodox in religion and used the Cyrillic alphabet, while the Croats were Roman Catholic and wrote in Latin characters. The Serbs were fighters; and after having secured their independence from Turkey, they led the drive for the union of all South Slavs. It was only natural that the Serbs, having suffered so much in the war, should feel that they had won independence and that they should play a major role in the new government. On the other hand, the Croats were richer and better educated than the Serbs and considered themselves culturally superior. The Serbs, who favored a unitary system, established a highly centralized regime; but the Croats, to whom autonomy had been for generations the most cherished weapon

11. For a discussion see B. W. Diffie and C. A. Thomson, "Spain Under the Republic," in R. L. Buell (ed.), *New Governments in Europe* (revised ed.; New York, 1937); F. E. Manuel, *The Politics of Modern Spain* (New York, 1938); Gerald Brenan, *The Spanish Labyrinth* (New York, 1943).

in the struggle for liberty against Hungary, never accepted the constitution and continued to favor a federal system. From 1919 to 1929 when King Alexander took over personal control there were twenty-three governments; and the history of this ten-year period is a long and dreary story of misunderstandings and complaints. As time went on, discussions in Parliament appeared to become more violent; and quarrels were marked by assassinations, enduring hatreds, obstruction, and the abstention of the Croats from Parliament. After a Serbian deputy murdered the leader of the Croat Peasant party in the assembly, the country experienced a complete breakdown in democratic government. The Croat deputies left Belgrade declaring that they would never again set foot in the existing Parliament, and the king found it impossible to find anyone who could form a government. Finally, King Alexander reluctantly decided to break the deadlock by declaring himself dictator.

The proletarian movement, which interestingly enough drew its leadership mainly from middle class intellectuals, has shown a tendency to split up into a number of factions; and this has contributed to the disruption of the basic unity upon which democracy depends. For example, one group tried to win control and achieve a socialist change through the parliamentary process, while another group held that nothing significant could be accomplished in this manner and advocated direct action. The parliamentary group, after it got into the legislature, divided over the strategy that ought to be followed. There were the reformists who supported measures like old age pensions and those who voted against them on the theory that they made capitalism work and thus gave it a longer life. The revolutionaries are further split on what means they should use when they get into power. For example, should the usual legislative procedure be used or should an enabling act be passed so that the government can rule by decree? There is also a division between the monist, who wants to capture control of the state and use the state to effect reform, and the pluralist who hates the idea of monistic organization and favors a stateless as well as a classless society. Although anarchism has never attracted much support, the syndicalist movement, which favors a society in which the state disappears and the means of production in each industry are owned, regulated, and completely controlled by those who are engaged in that branch of production, has been strong in a number of Latin countries, especially France, Italy, Spain, and Portugal. In this connection it is interesting to note that bolshevism thought in terms of monism for the time being and the ultimate establishment of a pluralist order. The effect of this process if it takes place within a weak state structure is that it tends to destroy the government and establish dictatorship.

Constitutionalism imposes limitations on the organs of government and diffuses powers in order to prevent a dangerous concentration at the top. This limitation may be enforced in a number of ways. For example, in some countries it is partially enforced by a supreme court which acts as the guardian of the constitution and repels encroachments by other agencies of the government. In other countries there are special administrative courts which prevent the executive from exceeding and abusing such powers as he has. Sometimes the existence of a federal system helps curtail and balance the powers of the central government, and sometimes this limitation is enforced by the different political groups which together exercise supreme guardianship in the legislature. However, in all countries reliance must ultimately be based upon a nation's sense of its heritage, upon a common understanding that certain things are not done, and upon an insistence that the time-honored procedure must be followed. In other words, all legal and theoretical rules rest on the expectation that every major group in the country will agree to be bound by the constitution and will not attempt to force its will beyond these limits. In the last analysis this agreement must be voluntary; for a state either collapses or becomes a dictatorship when a considerable number of people refuse to accept the constitution.

A voluntary agreement of this kind is possible only when the contending political forces within a country are not too far apart on fundamental principles. This does not mean that there cannot be spirited debates over important issues for the electorate to decide; but when mutual animosity and differences of opinion reach the point "where one political party feels that its very life is threatened by the possible victory of another important party, then constitutional barriers are easily brushed aside and the grim struggle for political, and sometimes physical, survival begins." [12]

12. Neumann, *European and Comparative Government*, p. 593.

POLITICAL INEXPERIENCE AND EXPLOITATION

It is impossible to operate a democratic government when the people are not interested in public affairs and when people have not had experience in self-government. There must be not only a passion for liberty but also a desire to preserve the conditions of liberty. This means that the people must possess enough of the common to sustain the common weal against the fierce conflicts of interests and factions. When class lines are strongly held and when a sense of class exploitation reaches deep into the masses of the population, democratic institutions are hard to establish and maintain. In Italy and Germany proportional representation made it possible for political parties representing narrow class interests to secure a larger representation in the legislature; and although political parties even in Germany did not have a strict class basis in the Marxian sense, they did tend to reflect narrow group interests and to develop platforms appealing to specific local, economic, or occupational interests to a much greater extent than in hardly any other country.[13]

Democracy repudiates the Marxian notion of class and class conflict. Although Marxian doctrine has frequently been democratic in its pretensions, it is nevertheless authoritarian in temper. This is because it seeks to overpower and eliminate the bourgeoisie; and since the bourgeoisie compose a considerable portion of the population, they inevitably resist by every means at their command. Marxist parties, unlike the Labor party in England, are not inclined to advocate a gradual approach to socialism.

> They oppose "reform" and believe in revolution. When they become powerful they regard the political conflict as a sheer struggle between themselves and the reactionary right, in which latter category they tend to include all who do not share their own allegiance. Marxism and fascism breed one another and in the clash, whichever wins, democracy loses.[14]

The situation that developed in Spain prior to the civil war is only one of many illustrations that could be given. Democracy puts the common interest, and not merely some majority interest, above the divisive interests of all groups.

Democracy requires a process of maturation. Where its spirit

13. Hermens, *Democracy or Anarchy?*, pp. 35–43, 241–244, 290–292.
14. MacIver, *The Web of Government*, p. 191.

has long been awake, as in Switzerland, Scandinavia, England, and the United States, the movement towards dictatorship has never succeeded. It may be that these countries were not so profoundly shaken by the universal crisis and that, if pressure had been further intensified, they too would have followed the same road. There are catastrophic conditions under which democracy cannot flourish or even endure. On the other hand, in immature republics, such as Weimar Germany, where there was no established democratic tradition, there was a greater willingness to follow the leader and to submit to authority. In these countries the people, faced with an economic and spiritual crisis, were more inclined to vote for political parties pledged to change not merely the government but the whole system of government.

DEMORALIZATION AND FEELING OF FUTILITY

Unfortunately the experiment in democratic government took place at an unfavorable time in most European countries. It was conducted amidst conditions of crisis and social unsettlement. The people were in a cynical and negative mood, and there was a feeling of insecurity in contrast to the more peaceful and settled conditions of the nineteenth century which permitted a slow and gradual adjustment to change. There was often an ignorant and inexperienced electorate, and the problems confronting these countries were of such magnitude that the people could not understand them.[15] Hence an attitude of pessimism replaced the optimism of

15. It is, of course, impossible to make up a checklist of the conditions for democracy and state with certainty that constitutional government is condemned to failure unless these factors are present in specific amounts. Professor Ferdinand A. Hermens, *Democracy or Anarchy?*, pp. 207–211, has shown that too great an emphasis has been placed upon literacy and education as a necessary condition for democracy and that many factors unfavorable to parliamentary institutions can be overcome by the integrating force supplied by a plurality system of election. India may prove to be an illustration of this point of view; for in the 1952 election the absence of proportional representation and the presence of an electoral system in which a plurality vote means victory made it possible for the Congress party to win a clear majority of the seats in Parliament with only 45 per cent of the popular vote. On the other hand, Myron Weiner, "Struggle Against Power: Notes on Indian Political Behavior," *World Politics*, VIII (April, 1956), 392–403, has correctly reminded us that "India's experiment with democratic institutions is still only an experiment." He calls attention to the absence of a basic consensus on the nature of the state, the lack of concern on the part of political leaders and their followers for the electoral consequences of their actions, civil disobedience, and the renunciation of political power as an objective by some groups. These and other traditional divisive factors, such as local caste

the nineteenth century. It was really more than not believing anything, i.e., not having a philosophy, although this was also an important factor as Peter Drucker shows.[16] It was in addition a feeling of being overwhelmed and not knowing which way to turn; and as conditions further deteriorated, there was a gradual undermining of faith in the regime and a feeling of despair among the masses. As a widespread feeling of the futility of parliamentary government increased, there was the positive demand for a redeemer or a leader to whom loyalties could be given.

Conditions such as these have often accompanied the rise of dictatorship in the past. No country can operate its state structure without a pattern of hope and without the feeling that the government can furnish a fulfillment of hope. For example, men will endure almost any kind of hardship so long as they believe that their children will enjoy things that they were unable to have. However, if there is a frustration of hope at every turn, the country is faced with a revolutionary situation; and when this feeling is widespread, there is the demand for a leader who will give them hope.

There is a tendency for men who are disappointed, frustrated, and discouraged to romanticize the past. As they thought about conditions existing before the upheavals brought about by the war, before the inflation, unemployment, and the desperate economic situation generally, before the terrible insecurity which was their present condition, they began to long for "the good old days." The more they thought about the past the more it became a virtual paradise in their minds. Although a return to the past was impossible and although the happy conditions imagined in their minds never existed, there was nevertheless a longing for the leader who will bring back "the good old days." Thus the repudiation of a regime can come from the right as well as from the left. In the United States and Britain there is no revolutionary movement from the right, but movements from the right can be every whit as

---

or language groups, have produced a fragmentation of Indian political life so that there are today "some fifty political parties with seats in either Parliament or the state assemblies." Although the working of the electoral system will undoubtedly compel minor parties to make compromises and merge with other groups, the survival of democratic government also depends upon the capacity of the parliamentary system to overcome traditional obstacles and create a more favorable environment for the operation of democratic institutions.

16. *The End of Economic Man* (New York, 1939).

dynamic as movements from the left. They do not spring merely from a few privileged groups; and if they were not popularly supported, they could not succeed.

SUMMARY

The liberal movement placed an emphasis on the sanctity of the individual and on rights, and hence it created an opportunity for those who wish to destroy the regime by granting freedom of speech and freedom of the press. Secondly, it assumed that there were certain postulates in regard to regime and that one knew the kind of court he would have to play the game; but the proletarian movement wanted to mark the court over again. There was still another repudiation of the liberal movement. Liberalism bases its hypothesis on the idea that problems can be solved by discussion and compromise; but a creed which believes in direct action tends to destroy the liberal movement as such. Most of the battles of the nineteenth century were merely shadow-boxing compared with the issues confronting society today. The most important questions debated in the nineteenth century—e.g., monarchy, the franchise, education, public health, the regulation of women's and children's labor, the place of churches in the state—were all matters which were easily understood and which were capable of a fairly simple solution. Today the issues confronting society are far more complicated, more difficult to dramatize, and less likely to be understood; yet the liberal movement presupposes that the individual knows what the choices are and that he will decide accordingly. Only recently have the unconscious assumptions upon which liberalism is based become apparent. The question arises as to whether these postulates of liberalism are merely a passing phenomenon which came out of a particular life and time and whether democracy is merely a system which has shown itself best adapted to a certain set of temporary conditions. History records a number of instances in which institutions are set up, modified, and abandoned, sometimes by the caprice of man and sometimes by the stern pressure of circumstances. It may be that there are forces now at work which will ultimately undermine the foundations of democracy.

The fundamental cleavages of society today cannot be compromised nor eliminated by an ingenious constitutional formula. The task confronting governments is to find a way whereby social conflicts can be resolved within the framework of the constitution. In addition, there must be a certain measure of economic stability; for a people driven to despair by deteriorating social and economic conditions are easily persuaded to adopt violent remedies. The future of democracy depends upon how successful the countries of the world are in fulfilling these tasks; for a failure to meet the problems of modern society in this manner probably means that efforts to resolve them will be made by regiments of soldiers on the battle field.

It is sometimes contended that history records no instance in which a ruling aristocracy has surrendered its power voluntarily and that a violent revolutionary expropriation of private property is necessary to induce the capitalist class to surrender the power and prestige which it now enjoys. It is, of course, true that no ruling class has ever surrendered its power voluntarily, but it does not follow that no ruling class has ever surrendered its power except under compulsion of naked force. For example, the English aristocracy under pressure exerted through democratic political procedure has conceded since the eighteenth century one strategic position after another. Moreover, the capitalist classes in all countries where democratic institutions still persist have gradually conceded much of the control over private property which they formerly possessed and which they once thought indispensable. There is no reason to assume that this process cannot continue in countries with a strongly intrenched democratic tradition or that a slow and progressive reform of almost any kind is impossible without incurring the destruction of democratic institutions.

The explanations given here for the rise of dictatorship are approximate only. In each country there were special conditions and particular factors which influenced the result and in each instance the total picture was different. Undoubtedly other factors could have been mentioned which are equally important. The reasons given are discernible to every one, for they are merely the outward manifestation of underlying causes. In every society there are obscure, underlying forces that act quite independently of the human will and shape the structure of human society. It remains for us to examine some of these underlying factors which have contributed to the rise of dictatorship.

THE CONSTITUTIONAL
INTERPRETATION

Even the most superficial study of history reveals that democracy has appeared at infrequent intervals and lasted only for brief periods of time. Civilization was already old when democracy made its first notable appearance among the small city states of ancient Greece. Here it flourished for only a century or two before it disappeared. For a thousand years, after the days of the last republicans of Rome, no one thought of trying to revive free self-government, and the most civilized peoples of Europe were ruled by their kings and chiefs. History quite clearly reveals that until recent times autocracy has been the predominant form of government, that the great majority of the human race has neither known nor much cared for representative institutions, and that in many of the countries where it has been tried democracy has had but a limited and temporary success.

About the middle of the nineteenth century democratic ideas began to spread from the more advanced nations of Western Europe to more backward areas. It was confidently expected that as industrialization and education increased autocratic governments would be superseded by democracy. Modern industry brought with it greater wealth; the increased wealth provided the possibility of better education; and education meant a more intelligent citizenry which would demand the right to participate in government. Even anti-democrats foresaw no limit to the spread of popular government.

If events in the nineteenth century revealed a trend towards a wider acceptance of representative institutions, it would appear that this trend has today been reversed. It was, of course, always true that democracy was loudly proclaimed in many places where it was not applied in practice; yet the contrast between the prestige, admiration, and respect representative institutions formerly enjoyed and the criticism and ridicule to which they are subjected today is a striking one. Moreover, many nations which had previously adopted a parliamentary regime have since rejected it.

Although it has been a common practice to attribute the spread of totalitarianism to the unscrupulous ambition of dictators, thoughtful democratic writers have been conscious of profounder causes. Violent changes do not occur without any reason. It is obviously impossible to account for the complete reversal of a previous tendency by a single simple explanation. The interplay of economic, intellectual, moral, and religious forces is perhaps more complex today than ever before, and hence it has become more difficult to diagnose the symptoms of our age. Nevertheless, it is obvious that there are forces at work in contemporary society which in many countries have sapped the democratic movement of its strength and vitality. In the long run, the revival of autocracy may be an aid to democratic government because it compels us to reëxamine the manner in which popular institutions can be improved and of the conditions under which they can best succeed. Although it is not possible to isolate the study of political institutions from that of other factors in the life of the community, emphasis in this chapter is placed upon the nature of constitutional development and the material conditions necessary for the successful operation of democracy.

NATURE OF CONSTITUTIONAL DEVELOPMENT

It has previously been pointed out that the modern nation state emerging at different times in various countries has passed or is passing through three main stages. Millions of people in the world today have not yet achieved national independence, have little political consciousness, and have not yet experienced the first phase. Others are in that stage, and many others are in the social service phase of development. Sir Ernest Barker, while pointing out the importance of a high degree of unity to governmental stability, made the following observation:

> Those of us who learned our history at the end of the nineteenth century were taught to think of the unification of Germany and Italy as if they were processes that had been already achieved in 1870. We now see that they were *not* achieved. They are still being achieved. The Führer and the Duce are the new Bismarck and the new Cavour of a new unification —a unification under the new and troublous conditions of a new social background. . . . We, who were unified long ago, cannot but deplore what to us are sad excesses of unitarian zeal—nowhere sadder, because nowhere more calculated and more doctrinaire, than they are in Germany, with its passion for the one Reich which is also one race and one religion. But just because we were unified long ago, in days when the majestic Henry VIII and the masterful Cromwell did their work upon us, we must also acknowledge that unity has to be won before stability can be found.[1]

But unification is today a long hard process—infinitely more difficult than in sixteenth century Britain—because in many countries a solution must be found not only for the political problems of unification but for serious social, economic, and religious controversies as well. The British people were indeed fortunate in having achieved national unification and having settled the religious controversy before the social and economic problems connected with the Industrial Revolution presented themselves. Being in agreement on the political and institutional structure of society, they can now proceed to disagree on social and economic policies. However, in many countries all of these things must be done at the same time. The result frequently is a chaotic party system which reflects the many possible combinations of opinion on these questions and an underlying disagreement concerning the basic contours of the state. Political stability is possible in a democratic system only after a high degree of unity has been achieved, and this has not yet come about in many countries of the world.[2]

1. Ernest Barker, *The Citizen's Choice* (London, 1937), pp. 83–84.
2. Professor Karl Loewenstein, "Autocracy versus Democracy in Contemporary Europe," *The American Political Science Review*, XXIX (1935), 586, says: "In all states which have been created as a result of the World War, national self-preservation may have warranted the adoption of a strong and stable government free from the dangers of party strife and devoted to the national reconstruction."

Some writers have contended that it is necessary to pass from the integral phase with its emphasis on unity into the liberal, or laissez-faire, stage before tackling the problems of the social service state. In some countries, notably in Italy and Germany, the transition has been from the integral directly to the social service phase without any time spent in the liberal period at all. The laissez-faire or liberal period has sometimes been called the legislative phase. For example, Ernest Barker calls it the period of "enthroned legislatures." [3] Today the demand is for strong and swift executive action and decision, but the constitutions of many countries were not set up for this sort of transition. They were set up for a different type of world and to deal with a different sort of problem. The result has been that the transition from a legislative to an executive state together with a crisis situation created too great a strain to be handled by democratic procedures.

There can be little doubt that conditions prevailing in the nineteenth century presented a more favorable environment for the operation of parliamentary institutions. The problems of government were simpler than they are today; public opinion was more homogeneous; agriculture was still the predominant occupation of men; and the representation of geographical areas had a meaning it has since lost. The electorate was then smaller, and an elaborate party organization was not needed. The issues discussed in the nineteenth century were of a character which the average man found interesting and intelligible without the possession of special knowledge, and lent themselves to eloquent debate in the legislature.[4]

Today the character of discussion has changed. It is indeed difficult to dramatize or to interest public opinion in matters such as the details of industrial reorganization, currency reform, grants-in-aid for housing, and other matters of this kind which require a special knowledge not available to the ordinary man. Moreover, as life becomes more technical and complicated it becomes increasingly difficult for legislators to understand thoroughly the details of the legislation concerning which they are called upon to pass; yet

3. Ernest Barker, *Reflections on Government* (London, 1942), pp. 94–100.
4. Professor Harold J. Laski, *Democracy in Crisis* (Chapel Hill, 1933), p. 70, says: "The debates of the nineteenth century did not, I think, arouse greater interest or secure wider publicity because their level was higher; it was rather because their subject matter was, in itself, calculated to arrest the attention of a non-technical audience."

the amount of legislation passed each year has increased to such an extent that representatives are overwhelmed with work and find it increasingly difficult to find the time for adequate discussion of legislative projects. The broad outlines of legislative procedure were laid down at a time when the main tasks of the state were few in number and negative in character. There was a suspicion of too much government, and legislative procedure developed forms which were designed to prevent a majority from riding roughshod over its opponents. Hence the amplitude of debate, the resentment of an assembly against steps designed to limit its initiative or freedom of discussion, and the power of a minister to make any question, no matter how insignificant, a question of confidence. Moreover, the very nature of political democracy precludes the possibility of swift and comprehensive action. Based as it is on a process of discussion, new measures cannot be undertaken until they have received the support of public opinion; a political party is naturally hesitant to promote novel ideas because of the possibility of defeat; and the number of interests to be consulted and the time required to do so is always great.

If parliamentary institutions arose in a period of relative calm and if they are better adapted to conditions prevailing in the liberal period than to the social service phase, nevertheless it is possible for an adjustment to be made if it can be done slowly and gradually enough to avoid too great a strain. Although the British constitution has maintained something of its essential and original character, it is at the same time flexible and elastic; and no picture of it in any one generation is wholly true of it in another. Thus it was possible for a tradition to develop together with a gradual adaptation of institutions to meet the changing needs of the changing times. However, on the Continent of Europe the democratic experiment was undertaken in a period of internal and international crisis when the need for swift and drastic action prevented the establishment of precedent and tradition.

Some writers have contended that the British Parliament never has been a body specially and primarily empowered to make laws. Its main task has never been to legislate or govern but to secure the full discussion of all matters, legislative or administrative, as the condition to giving its assent to bills or its support to ministers. Although the function of legislation is shared among "King, Lords, and Commons in Parliament assembled," it has always been predominantly exercised by government which, indeed, has never allowed Parliament as such to take any initiative in one of its most important fields, that of finance. Thus the mainspring of action has always been the government and the first consideration has always been the formation of a government as such.[5]

Whatever the validity of this view may be from an historical standpoint, it must be admitted that this is the principle upon which the British system operates today. The primary purpose of Parliament is not to govern or even to legislate; it is instead to furnish an effective majority ready to support a fairly coherent policy and to educate public opinion through discussion. However, in the nineteenth century a number of British writers, influenced by the then dominant Liberal individualist school, interpreted the parliamentary situation of their own time as a system based on the delegation of authority by the electorate to a Parliament which, in turn, delegated the day-by-day exercise of that power to a cabinet. Thus Bagehot referred to the cabinet as only a committee of the parliamentary majority, and not one of the eighteen chapters of Mill's *Representative Government* is devoted to the functions of the cabinet.

The little real importance that writers in this period assigned to the part played by the Crown, as embodied officially in the cabinet, fits in peculiarly with conditions prevailing in England at that time. The absence of any serious external menace and the *laissez-faire* theories of the age in economic matters reduced the work of both administration and legislation to a minimum. The result was that parliamentary debate dominated the attention of the public because

5. L. S. Amery, *Thoughts on the Constitution* (London, 1947), pp. 11–32. "It is the Government which, in the name of the Crown, makes appointments and confers honours without consulting Parliament. It is the Government, in the name of the Crown, which summons Parliament. It is the Government which settles the programme of parliamentary business and directs and drives Parliament in order to secure that programme. If Parliament fails to give sufficient support it is the Government, or an alternative Government, which, in the name of the Crown, dissolves Parliament. At a general election the voter is not in a position to choose either the kind of representative or the kind of government he would like if he had a free choice. There is a Government in being which he can confirm or else reject in favour of the alternative team. The candidates before him—the only candidates worth taking seriously—are either supporters of the team in office or of its rivals for office. It is within those narrow limits that his actual power is exercised." *Id.* at pp. 15–16. See also W. Ivor Jennings, *Cabinet Government* (Second edition; London, 1951).

a few broad issues of policy could be spread over prolonged and eloquent debates. Both parties and the electorate were drawn from a limited social stratum; and the almost evenly balanced and little disciplined Parliament of the time frequently upset the government. From these facts it was easy to conclude that Parliament was in fact the body which governed and did so in response to the wishes of an actively interested electorate.

It was this conception of the British constitution which was transplanted to the Continent of Europe. Here the paramount concern was to control the permanent administrative staff. In fact, the dislike of the French public for the civil service found expression in the epithet "bureaucracy," which is still so widely used today. Throughout the nineteenth century the main target of attack was the long-established dominance of this centralized bureaucracy; and the history of representative government is concerned chiefly with efforts to bring this specialized bureaucracy under parliamentary control. The place of the executive was depressed because memories of an old and indigenous regime of executive absolutism inspired a fear of its ambitions, and an omnipotent legislature watched with a jealous eye the operation of the new and diminished executive in order to prevent its reversion to the old type. This attitude, which is typical of French liberalism, prevented the emergence of well-integrated executive leadership. It reproduced the outward form of the British constitution without its spirit of strong and stable government, and it has almost everywhere broken down. By its nature it is bound to be weak and unstable, subject as it is to the continuous shifting and reshuffling of coalition ministries and to the influence of personal ambitions. The rise of dictatorships and of one-party governments has been the almost inevitable consequence of the ineffectiveness of such constitutions which have been unable to cope with the growing need for more governmental action and more definite leadership.

In Britain the progressive extension of the franchise and the continuous increase in the volume of government work led in the latter part of the nineteenth century to a stronger party organization in the country and to stricter party discipline in Parliament. These factors, together with a two-party system, has had the effect of strengthening the executive to such an extent that today the initiative has passed almost completely to the cabinet. Since Britain was the home of liberalism, she was able to make a slow and gradual adjustment in her institutions so as to be better able to meet the demands of the welfare state. Moreover, a strong tradition had become established which had to be only gradually modified in practice because a long period of laissez-faire guaranteed a slow and gradual adjustment to change. It is those countries in which liberalism lasted longest that have been most successful in making the necessary adjustments to contemporary conditions without a resort to dictatorial rule.

NATURE OF THE PARTY SYSTEM

It has sometimes been said that "nothing reveals so much the nature of a country as its system of political parties." Institutions provide the environment and framework within which parties must operate and thus help determine the scope of political activity. On the other hand, a detailed and systematic study of a country's party system will provide all the essential facts to fill in a broad outline of its institutional system. A parliamentary system requires parties if it is to work. They organize the chaotic public will, educate the electorate by providing conflicting opinions, and serve as a connecting link between government and public opinion. However, perhaps the most important reason for the rise of dictatorship has been the failure to develop a satisfactory party system.

The danger of a multiple party system in which it is difficult to ascertain the will of the majority or to maintain a stable combination of groups has already been pointed out. Under such a system responsibility is not made definite, party stalemate may prevent the executive from taking constructive action, and the legislature is prevented from representing public opinion sufficiently to do anything at all. Under these circumstances, a populace faced with a crisis situation will demand someone who can do something even if he has to rule by decree. This is a fairly accurate description of the situation prevailing in both Italy and Germany before the rise of Mussolini and Hitler. It is interesting to note that dictatorship has not come to a single country in Europe which had a democratic executive strong enough to govern.

In recent years a great deal of thought has been given to the problem of strengthening the executive. One school of thought tends to emphasize the importance of the power of the executive to effect a dissolution of parliament. It is argued that the power of the executive to force an election strengthens the cabinet against parliament and eliminates irresponsible criticism. This theory has been particularly popular in France where it has been used to explain why British governments are stable and French governments are not. It was the argument used by Premier Doumergue during the constitutional crisis of 1934, and it is still popular in France today. However, it is by no means certain that the power of dissolution would in itself strengthen the executive of that country to any appreciable extent. Dissolution is useless unless it breaks the deadlock and produces a different result. It was frequently used in Weimar Germany, but it did not increase executive stability. This was because new elections brought only slight shifts and because the post-election coalition governments were often very much like those which preceded them. The power of the British executive is due to party discipline operating within the framework of a two-party system and depends only to a very limited extent on the right to dissolve. Opposition members obey their leader, who could not plunge them into a general election if they rebelled, quite as regularly as government supporters obey the Prime Minister. In both cases they do so because they are persuaded either through conviction or through dislike of the other side. Moreover, recalcitrants are coerced through fear of opposition by an official party candidate at the next election. Although the threat of dissolution is still an important weapon for restoring discipline within the party and bringing wavering members into line, it is no longer the main factor making for the power of the executive in Great Britain.

An effective power of dissolution would not automatically transform French politics and politicians into the image of their British counterparts; but it might have a beneficial effect upon the working of French government. This is because ministries are often defeated for small and petty reasons. Although making dissolution easier would not in itself revolutionize the party system and establish a really coherent majority, it might promote ministerial stability by influencing marginal votes in critical divisions.[6]

It has sometimes been said that the disastrous establishment of a

6. For a discussion of the power of dissolution see Philip Williams, *Politics in Post-War France* (New York, 1954), pp. 225–233; Duverger, *Political Parties*, pp. 206–207, 404–405.

myriad of parties was furthered by the proportional system of election. There are many different systems of PR and the results, therefore, are somewhat different according to the type used and the method adopted in applying the proportional principle. However, almost everywhere the result has been to create an environment favorable to small parties even if it has not increased their number. Although the Weimar Republic began operations with only ten political parties in the legislature, as time went on there was a tendency for their number to increase.[7] Thus in a country already suffering from the absence of basic intellectual and sentimental unity, an electoral system was established under which new and extreme parties could multiply and render the fabric of politics even more fragile. Social and economic particularism was encouraged so that each of the parties tended to become identified with a special interest group, and special interests organized parties of their own. The multiple-member constituency tended to isolate the electorate from the representative whom it had chosen and thus to prevent an easy contact and interplay between them. The list system insured a tight control by the party bosses, a rigidity of party lines, and a disregard for the marginal voter. Whatever proportional representation may be capable of becoming under conditions less passionately partisan, it did not tend to mitigate the passions of conflicting parties but served to exacerbate them. Although proportional representation prevented swollen majorities and attenuated minorities, it did nothing to produce a spirit of compromise among the parties and tended to encourage a programmatic dogmatism which is inconsistent with parliamentary government. If the goal of an electoral system is not merely to reflect public opinion but also to permit the formation of a parliamentary majority capable of governing and to create a government, then the Weimar system does not qualify.

For a number of years Professor Ferdinand A. Hermens has been studying the theoretical and practical aspects of electoral sys-

7. "In the elections to the Weimar Assembly, 10 party lists secured representation and 19 did not; in the Reichstag elections of May, 1928, 15 parties secured representation and 23 did not; and in the Reichstag elections of September, 1930, 16 parties secured seats and 21 did not. In a decade, therefore, the parties represented in the German legislature increased by more than 50 per cent and the number offering lists in the elections increased by more than 27 per cent." A. J. Zurcher, *The Experiment with Democracy in Central Europe* (New York, 1933), pp. 85–86. See also Herbert Kraus, *The Crisis of German Democracy* (Princeton, 1932), pp. 137–154.

tems, and his conclusions concerning the effects of proportional representation upon political behavior draw attention to a factor which contributed significantly to the rise of modern dictatorship.[8] His analysis shows that almost everywhere the result has been to create an environment favorable to small parties and to increase the difficulty in finding a majority to support a government. In the United States and Great Britain the maintenance of a two-party system is mainly the result of an electoral system which discourages small parties, but the government is nevertheless sensitive to minority interests because each major party must secure the support of as many different groups as possible to win elections. Under these circumstances party programs are moderate and not doctrinaire, and elections serve as an expression of the popular will. Even under a two-ballot system specially designed for countries having a multi-party system, as in France under the Third Republic, elections supply an integrating force because such a system encourages the formation of blocs during the campaign which can cohere reasonably well after the election is over.

Proportional representation, on the other hand, has a divisive effect and contributes to governmental instability. This is partially because it encourages the formation of small parties and splinter groups; but even when restrictive features are added to limit the number of small parties, it creates an atmosphere which destroys national unity and hinders the formation of governments with solid parliamentary support. This is because under the list system political parties are free to campaign on their own programs without taking into consideration the views of other parties or groups. Such a system is made to order for parties inclined to take doctrinaire positions and representing narrow class or group interests; for the electoral system does not compel them to modify their positions and cooperate with other groups. They are instead "free" to be as dogmatic as they wish and to cultivate their own clientele. Instead of an expression of opinion emanating from elections there are only a conglomeration of unrelated groups representing narrow interests and taking varied positions on the most important questions. Such

8. See particularly his *Democracy or Anarchy? A Study of Proportional Representation* (Notre Dame, 1941) and *Europe Between Democracy and Anarchy* (Notre Dame, 1951). The earlier volume has recently been published in Germany, *Demokratie oder Anarchie? Untersuchung über die Verhältniswahl* (Frankfurt A. M., 1951).

a system has made more difficult than ever before the formation of cabinets. This is partly because under PR the number of parties to be taken into consideration has a tendency to increase; but even more important than the number of parties is the fact that political groups which have campaigned on the basis of a narrow party program cannot readily enter into the compromises necessary to form a government. Moreover, the electoral system has a profound effect upon the psychology of the voter. Although it has become fashionable in most countries to blame scheming and ambitious politicians for governmental instability and although the average American tends to view prolonged cabinet crises and the reluctance of politicians to make the obvious compromises necessary to form a government as cases of political stupidity, the truth of the matter is that politicians dare not make the necessary bargains too readily. Since the political parties hold tenaciously to certain philosophies and since they campaign during elections exclusively on the basis of their own principles, they cannot readily compromise them after the election without running the risk of losing popular support. Under these circumstances a cabinet crisis becomes soluble only when the whole country is exasperated and when the political parties are in danger of losing more support by following a policy of intransigence than in reaching agreement.

An atmosphere, therefore, is created which is favorable to extremist parties. The weakness of the government and its incapacity to make decisions disgusts the citizenry, and the general frustration breeds an attitude of contempt for parliamentary institutions. Communist and fascist groups, which would have been defeated or severely reduced in representation under a majority system, are able to capitalize on the situation and increase their support. When a country reaches a political stalemate dictatorship cannot be far away; for nature abhors a vacuum and freedom cannot exist without authority. Although it would be an exaggeration to say that the baneful effects of the electoral system were alone responsible for the rise of dictatorship, Professor Hermens thinks that in both Italy and Germany proportional representation might well have been "the decisive factor." [9] Even in Belgium, Holland, Switzerland, and the Scandinavian countries, which are frequently cited to prove that proportional representation need not lead to the unfortunate results

9. *Democracy or Anarchy?*, pp. 198–213, 285–300.

it has produced in other states, Professor Hermens has demonstrated that it supplied a disruptive influence and that results would have been better under a majority system of voting.[10]

Although proportional representation has the appearance of being more democratic in the sense that each party is awarded representation roughly on the basis of its electoral support, such a system is not in fact sensitive to public opinion. This is because elections do not as a rule record a swing of the pendulum but generally produce approximately the same results. Since the system encourages voters to support the party of their choice and to cling tenaciously to their opinions, the element of compromise, which is essential to the democratic process, must be supplied after the election is over; and the bargains worked out by parliamentarians may be along lines which the voters would never have approved if they had been in a position to exercise a choice. Moreover, under the list system the deputy is not in close contact with his constituents but is under the domination of the party bosses. This is because PR requires a large multi-member district for elections, because the voter casts his ballot for a party rather than a candidate, and because party leaders determine the candidates and the order in which their names appear on the ballot.

Cabinet government apparently works best when there is a two-party system because the cabinet has a clear and stable majority in parliament for which it is the leader and spokesman. One of the principal reasons for the emergence of dictatorship has been the inability of parliamentary regimes to provide effective leadership and a definite governmental program. An adequate electoral system can help produce agreement by emphasizing the forces making for integration just as proportional representation emphasizes factors which make for disintegration. It is not the existence of a multiparty system which makes for instability but the underlying cleavages in the country. For example, Austria came as close to developing a two-party system as any country on the Continent of Europe; but although the Socialists and Christian Democrats controlled between four-fifths and nine-tenths of the seats, a system of proportional representation prevented either party from winning a majority.[11] Moreover, Austrian parties failed to develop a spirit of toler-

10. *Ibid.*, pp. 301–311, 331–355.
11. Hermens, *Europe Between Democracy and Anarchy*, pp. 83–86.

ance and the willingness to compromise which are so essential to the successful operation of democracy. In the last analysis, there must be a certain degree of moderation among the parties. There must be an agreement upon fundamental matters and a willingness to compromise on others. If the parties are not too far apart, the opposition understands and observes the rules of the game as the majority party does; but when one party feels deeply that life and liberty are gravely endangered if its opponents gain the upper hand, then orderly government becomes very difficult. The result is likely to be that such a party will follow a policy of obstruction and that if this fails force will eventually be applied. Under such circumstances orderly government comes to an end; emergency decrees take the place of legislative acts; and from this point on, it is only a step to dictatorship.

The totalitarian parties of today have grown up within the democratic party system and have merely accentuated characteristics already found in the party system long before they ever came to power. In contrast to the American and British approach, where political issues tend to revolve around practical concrete proposals, continental parties tend to have distinct political philosophies and ideological concepts with which they attempt to imbue their followers. This devotion to theory and well-defined political principles overshadowed the day-to-day routine of parliamentary life and occupied a central position in electoral campaigns and party propaganda. On the Continent of Europe class distinctions have been preserved; and although few parties can afford to be pure class parties, they do tend to have a class basis. In most of these countries basic questions concerning the form of government were not settled before the Industrial Revolution transformed society, and a basic disagreement on fundamental principles was thus carried into our times. In France the atmosphere of debate still reflects the bitter memories of street fighting and the depth of political passion which has led that country through civil wars. In Germany history and tradition provided an absolute temper and doctrinaire spirit which made the parties uncompromising and intractable. This is partially because they grew up within the old authoritarian system and were an inheritance of the old pre-war absolutist regime rather than built into a system of democratic institutions. Under the Empire they stood on the circumference of an alien system and were deprived of any chance for responsibility. Being isolated and deprived of the moderating effects of responsibility, they developed a spirit of programmatic dogmatism and isolated themselves still further. Unfortunately this attitude was carried over to the Weimar Republic where it was greatly augmented by proportional representation. This is because the list system concentrated all attention on the parties as entities and consequently on their doctrines. Such a system led to brilliant theorizing, and interparty argument was often an interesting affair. However, it did little to encourage a spirit of moderation among the parties; for compromise is frequently possible only when concrete measures, rather than abstract theories, are discussed.

The result was a change in the conception of party and the role it should play in the community. Instead of discussing issues and policies and serving as an educator of the electorate, the parties sought to control and dominate the electorate. Instead of an appeal to reason on concrete issues, they sought to become philosophers of life and to mold all life into the image of their philosophies. Instead of serving as organs for the measured debate of opinion, they considered themselves as armies preparing for a conflict in the nature of civil war. This is particularly true of the Marxist parties, but it was also true of other parties as well. When parties thus become total, there is, in the last analysis, only room for one; and when one party triumphs under these circumstances, the state becomes "totalitarian." The Communist, Fascist, and National Socialist parties were the culmination of a totalitarian tendency which had begun even in the late nineteenth century.

This changed conception of party has had a profound effect upon party organization. In both England and the United States party organization has grown tremendously from the time when the parties were loose bodies of common opinion or voluntary clubs with an informal organization and scanty financial resources.[12] Today there are paid and permanent managers, the local organizations with their officers and members, the professional politicians, research bureaus, workers, and organizers. This is an inevitable

---

12. For a discussion of the growth of party organization in England, see A. L. Lowell, *Government of England* (New York, 1909), I, 466–570; and R. T. McKenzie, *British Political Parties* (London, 1955).

development which has been brought about by the growth of the great electorate and the increased business and prolonged sessions of the legislature which have made the work of the representative a full-time job. Governmental intervention in social and economic affairs has stimulated a larger interest and more activity because the stakes are greater. However, in both Britain and the United States party organization has centered its attention primarily on appealing directly to the voter and getting him to the polls on election day; but political parties may attempt to do much more than wage campaigns and organize supporters in order to win elections. They may seek to engulf the lives of their members and provide them with party trade unions, party sports clubs, and party methods of education, and a general party apparatus of life.

One finds this tendency to some extent even in England; but it was nowhere carried further than in Weimar Germany. Here the German genius for organization manifested itself not only in national, regional, district, and precinct headquarters with party sections holding periodic meetings and some educational work going on all of the time but also in a myriad of affiliated organizations as well. Thus the individual party member could have his entire personal and much of his professional life within the confines of a particular party. For example, a socialist worker could buy his groceries at the Social Democratic cooperative, send his children to a Social Democratic school, belong to a socialist union, and hold membership in a socialist burial society, sports club, and reading circle. He would, of course, read the party press in which news unfavorable to the party was either suppressed or slanted. Speeches delivered by the party's representatives in the Reichstag were reported in great detail but the arguments of opposing speakers were completely ignored or else it was merely mentioned that they spoke. Every opportunity was provided for the individual willing to do so to relinquish his power of decision and to lose his individuality in party activity. There were organizations for every conceivable activity depending upon the individual's interests and economic status. In addition to the groups already mentioned, there were socialist hiking clubs, youth groups, women's organizations, chess federations, special socialist organizations for doctors, students, commercial employees, small business men, and many others. Anyone interested in the ramifications of this elaborate organization need only to consult a few past or present issues of the party press to see the extent to which party activity can dominate a man's whole life.

Although the examples given here apply to the Social Democrats, other political parties also perfected a similar organization. Organization and activity on such a scale obviously foster a spirit of exclusiveness which leads to more cleavage in the population. Party members tend to speak a different language, live according to a different set of values, develop a comradely spirit, and view their opponents as barely human. In a word, the party becomes a "state within the state." Although such activity may appeal to the gregarious instinct in man and give him a fuller social life, it can hardly be expected to improve his judgment or increase his powers of critical evaluation.

A democratic party system is based upon the idea that man is a rational animal capable of intelligent choice and that, having heard the arguments, he will make a wise decision; but when emotion takes the place of reason, when party organization reaches the point where party spirit completely dominates his mind, or when there is no longer the possibility that he will exercise a choice, then the democratic process tends to break down. It is undoubtedly true that the number of independent voters who record the general movements of opinion by changing their votes from time to time is always small; but party organization can become so intensive that it precludes a reasonable opportunity for all groups to appeal to the electorate and to influence its judgment by intellectual argument. Under such circumstances the electorate tends to become fixed in its allegiances and inflexible in its attitudes. There can be no swing of the pendulum but a constant stalemate with the added threat of civil war. The cry is then heard for a party above parties, for a "movement" which will encompass all others and bring about a "new unity."

Democracy is based upon the assumption that the party can penetrate the associations to which an individual belongs, that it can teach its programmes, and that the individual will consider the alternatives with an open mind; but the total party attempts to indoctrinate its members thoroughly, to cover the whole of men's minds, and to mold their minds so as to leave them in no position to exercise a free choice. When parties become emotional absolutes, they cease to be a part of the system of rational discussion.

DIFFICULTY OF ESTABLISHING DEMOCRACY

There is a high infant mortality to young democracies. Democracy requires a long period of maturation and growth and fails where it has been denied. In England parliamentary institutions have been developing for at least seven hundred years. Democratic representation was not achieved at a single stroke but only very slowly and gradually. As a matter of fact, a genuine universal suffrage dates only from 1928 when all adult women were finally admitted to the franchise. The gradual extension of the suffrage throughout the nineteenth century meant that new voters could be absorbed and obtain a measure of experience and political education before new recruits were added to the electorate. As the people slowly gained control of the government, they grew up to their responsibilities. Since the machinery of government involved institutions which the people had made for themselves, they learned in making them how to operate them successfully. As the government gradually became more complex and complicated, their increasing experience taught them how to handle it. Thus democracy in Britain was a gradual growth and took its form as the result of a long series of adaptations to emergent conditions and needs.

In many countries, however, an attempt is being made to cover the same ground in a single generation. By a sudden stroke the masses without previous political experience are called upon to work the vast and elaborate organization of a great modern state and perform tasks which in other countries it has taken centuries of struggle and training to accomplish. When free institutions are forced upon a people who have not spontaneously called for them, they come as something not only unfamiliar but also artificial. Thus in many countries democracy has been more formal than real. This was particularly true of Italy where representative institutions were superimposed by a small Liberal élite and never penetrated society deeply. A hard-working and economically depressed citizenry divided by geographical barriers and by strong regional and local attachments failed to develop a nation-wide party system, and political life was dominated by a small group of *politicos* who depended more upon a personal than upon a party following in Parliament. Thus in spite of the semblance of democratic elections "statesmanship was reduced to a veiled dictatorship, depending for a day-to-day existence upon the adroit manipulation of coalition majorities in an atmosphere of intrigue, fraud, and violence." [13]

A people cannot bring democracy into immediate existence by a sudden change of attitude. This is why the infant mortality of new democracies is always high. The struggle of a new democracy to survive against the forces of the old order is usually long and hard, as the history of France abundantly shows. After its initiation French democracy several times fell and rose again. Even today there are still powerful groups who challenge the republic, who are opposed to the ideals of the French Revolution, and who consider it and everything it stood for a supreme mistake. When a country has been accustomed to a more authoritarian government, it is difficult to introduce a democratic regime, and certainly no borrowed scheme can be abruptly thrust upon a people who have not been in any way prepared for the responsibilities of self-government.

Imperial Germany and Austria-Hungary had constitutions and the people lived under regimes in which power was not wielded arbitrarily but generally according to law (*Rechtsstaat*). However, public opinion was given no opportunity to exercise an effective control over government, and the people were ruled by a political bureaucracy which was rooted in the old traditional forces of aristocracy, plutocracy, and the army. Although the regime provided efficient government, the people themselves were denied an opportunity to secure experience in self-government. When they were later suddenly transferred from the benevolent paternalism of a semi-absolutist government to the possession of free democratic institutions, there was little in the way of a democratic tradition on which to build. Although government under the monarchy was by no means as autocratic as under fascism, still a subsequent return to authoritarian rule did not mean the loss of a traditional freedom and the denial of precious rights for which their fathers had fought and died. Democracy was not an indispensable part of their national history. The same could be said of Spain, the Balkan states, and the newly

13. F. A. Ogg, *European Governments and Politics* (Second edition; New York, 1939), p. 814.

created states of post-war democracy. In none of these countries was dictatorship established after representative government had had a sufficiently long period of trial for a democratic tradition to develop and for the bulk of the people to become acquainted with the advantages of self-government as compared with the autocratic rule they had formerly enjoyed.

MATERIAL CONDITIONS FOR DEMOCRACY

Democracy is a delicate form of government which rests upon conditions that are rather precarious. It makes certain assumptions about the capacities and virtues of men, and it presumes the presence of certain material and intellectual conditions favorable to the exercise of these capacities and virtues. John Stuart Mill, whose devotion to liberty cannot be doubted, pointed out that a people might desire liberty and yet be unable or unwilling to fulfill its conditions.[14] There must be a wide range of interest and a capacity to relate one's own immediate interest to a more general pattern. The only possible government is some kind of oligarchy when people are deeply divided by racial, religious, or other differences. When oligarchy or autocracy are removed from on top of racial or other differences, there is a tendency for group interests to assert themselves and to demand autonomy. When the majority are unable to share in the benefits of communal life, when the struggle for existence is too great, when all of a man's energy is used up in eking out a bare subsistence and remaining alive, it becomes impossible to operate a democratic system. This is why in modern times there has been such a close association between democracy and industrial development. Not all rich industrial states have shown a tendency to develop democratic constitutions, and early America provides an illustration of representative government operating successfully in an agrarian society. However, a predominantly immobile agricultural society, which is at the same time very poor, is not likely to develop a democratic form of government. Democracy cannot succeed when intense social unsettlement prevails, as, for example, in Rumania, Greece, Portugal, and particularly in South America today. As R. M. MacIver has pointed out, "The form of govern-

14. See his *Representative Government* (Everyman's Library; New York, 1936), esp. pp. 175–184, 218–227.

ment is always a reflection of underlying social attitudes, even though the reflection is sometimes belated." [15]

It is sometimes contended that democracy means the rule of the majority or the rule of the masses. This was the interpretation given by the Greek philosophers before there was a representative system or a party system, and it helps explain why on the whole they disapproved of it. The most intolerant and the most anti-democratic of governments may receive mass support. It is possible that a greater proportion of the citizens support or have supported the Soviet or Nazi regime than in this country favor the present administration in Washington. A dictatorship may also rest on a majority will, and democracy is not the only form of government which secures mass support. However, a democracy gives free-play to opinion, and it presupposes that all are prepared to accept, even if they do not approve, the majority decision. It follows that there are certain issues which are so divisive in their nature that they ought never to be put to a vote.

In the United States and England it is generally conceded that not only the majority but also the minority have rights. One of the principal aims of the framers of our Constitution was to check majority rule; and although in England there are no constitutional restrictions, nevertheless the spirit of the constitution implies that the majority should not deal with the minority in an arbitrary manner and that all Englishmen have certain rights. It would appear that this is an indispensable condition for the successful operation of democracy; for a minority about to be stripped of its "rights" will use force to protect its position. In other words, the policy of the government must be moderate. Every group or interest must feel that it has a "fighting chance" to influence the government and that while the opposition is in power that everything worthwhile in life will not be destroyed.

By its very nature democracy guarantees a gradual, rather than a rapid, adjustment to new conditions. This is because democracy, as majority-rule, must not adopt measures which will permanently alienate a large class or group. Thus there are certain issues which ought never to be put to a vote because they could not be adopted without stirring up a bitter antagonism which would threaten the democratic system itself. For example, it is anti-democratic to pro-

15. *The Web of Government,* p. 191.

pose an immediate transfer of the prevailing profits-system into a socialist order, not because of the intrinsic merits or demerits of the proposal itself, but because it could not be done without the abandonment of democratic principles.[16] Those who propose an immediate revolution in the economic order and at the same time advocate the retention of democratic liberties are either insincere or else ignorant of the principles upon which democracy is based. This does not mean that it is impossible for democracies to undertake large schemes of economic reconstruction or that a democratic state may not make a considerable transformation of a capitalist economy if public opinion runs long enough and strong enough in that direction. However, in a democracy the people must become habituated to new ideas and conscious of new needs before new institutions are created. On the other hand, dictatorship has frequently been the swift solution of an emergency and the means by which an old order is destroyed and a new one set in its place.

CONCLUSION

Democracy presupposes the production of a certain type of man, and circumstances may operate in such a way as to prevent the production of that type of man. The attitude of a given people and their standards of value are the result of their experience, and circumstances may prevent in a given community the development of a democratic spirit. It follows that there is no "best" or "ideal" form of government. The best form is that which is best adapted to the particular circumstances of a given state at a particular stage of its political development. Aristotle long ago observed that "political writers, although they have excellent ideas, are often unpractical" and pointed out that the "true legislator and statesman ought to be acquainted, not only with that form of government which is best in the abstract, but also that which is best relatively to circumstances. . . . There is certainly more than one form of democracy and of oligarchy; nor are the same laws equally suited to all." [17]

Of all forms of government parliamentary democracy is the most delicate requiring for its operation the greatest experience and the highest technical skill. It was absurd to imagine that the Greeks,

16. See Gerhard Colm, "Is Economic Planning Compatible with Democracy?" in Max Ascoli and Fritz Lehmann (eds.), *Political and Economic Democracy* (New York, 1937), pp. 21–41.

17. *Politics,* Bk. IV, Ch. 1.

having been suddenly emancipated from the domination of the Ottoman Empire after centuries of subjection, could make a success of parliamentary democracy right away. In England the local courts of the Shire, the Hundred, and the Township were the training ground for the knights and burgesses who were summoned in the thirteenth century to a central representative assembly to make their grants to the Crown. Parliament was in continuous existence for at least four centuries, doing the work of legislation and taxation, before it was entrusted with the control of a responsible executive. The breakdown of premature experiments, where the people have not undergone a prolonged apprenticeship, ought not to excite surprise or even less contempt. A little more reflection upon these facts should also help avoid the common tendency to prescribe for others constitutional arrangements like our own and make us more restrained in our criticism of contemporary experiments in government.

In terms of our experience democracy has been extremely successful. Because of this fact, a host of loyalties surround the word, and to Americans democracy means something eminently desirable and the highest good that a people can attain. It may very well be that in other societies, where democracy has not achieved much success, that the people will have a different standard of values. Democracy, for example, may be associated with defeat and an unpleasant experience in their national life. As a result, they are likely to consider democracy synonymous with evil rather than good, to believe that it means a weak government incapable of meeting the needs of present-day society, and to feel that it is something to be avoided rather than achieved.

THE ECONOMIC CRISIS

IN ANY society there is bound to be a close relationship between economic and political power. All human activity has an economic aspect; the most persistent problems of any government are economic problems; and interest has in general been focused more upon the "economic causes" of dictatorship than upon any other single factor. It has long been recognized that the dissatisfactions arising from unemployment, depression, inflation, and economic dislocations generally have played an important role in the demand for a change of regime. The failure of governments because of executive impotence and party stalemate to deal effectively with the economic crisis and the resulting demand for a leader who would provide strong and effective government have already been mentioned as important reasons for the failure of democracy and the rise of dictatorship. However, many observers, struck by the close relationship of economic and political power, have attempted to explain the rise of dictatorship in terms of the distribution of property, class conflict, and class support.

ECONOMIC THEORIES OF DICTATORSHIP

1. The Marxian explanation. Perhaps the most popular explanation for the rise of dictatorship has been derived from Marxian philosophy. According to this view, every state has a class basis. Political democracy, therefore, is nothing more than a concealed dictatorship which permits the capitalists to delude the workers;

and so long as it can be carried on it is, from the capitalist point of view, the most efficient and acceptable form of government. However, the growth of working-class organizations and universal suffrage have produced a clash between the working-class and the owners of property, and the capitalist is compelled to resort to open force to maintain his position. Thus fascism is an effort to save capitalism and give it a longer life by preventing the establishment of socialism. "The creation of a fascist party is, then, a desperate expedient only resorted to by a capitalist class in the face of the most urgent danger from the workers." [1]

Although perhaps only the most confirmed Marxist would accept this interpretation, there is a tendency on the part of many writers to regard dictatorship as in some way the rule of a social class. This idea is compatible with all sorts of refinements. For example, it has been contended that monopoly capitalism inevitably leads to dictatorship [2] and that National Socialism and Italian Fascism were the governments of large capitalists because the measures undertaken after they came to power benefited the industrialists, bankers, and large landowners. [3]

2. Polarization of an authoritarian left and right. It has also been contended that certain conditions inherent in democracy itself create an anti-democratic spirit and that as time goes on there is a tendency for the adherents of democracy to decrease and for the supporters of dictatorship to increase. This is because the left develops a fear of majority rule believing that if the decision were left to the ballot box that they would lose. There is no government more conservative than a democratic regime because the people are by nature suspicious of change and because drastic reforms cannot be undertaken until the great body of the people have become convinced of the need for change. The result is that the left begins to despair of winning a majority at the polls and the demand for and a readiness to accept a dictatorship on the Russian pattern are greatly enhanced. On the other hand, the middle classes also fear majority rule because it means the enthronement of the "have-nots." With the development of communication and education, there is a

1. John Strachey, *The Coming Struggle for Power* (New York, 1933), p. 262; see also by the same author, *The Menace of Fascism* (New York, 1933).
2. Robert A. Brady, *Business as a System of Power* (New York, 1943).
3. Robert A. Brady, *The Spirit and Structure of German Fascism* (New York, 1937); R. Palme Dutt, *Fascism and Social Revolution* (New York, 1935).

constant increase in the number of people whose ideas are anti-democratic. Out of this situation will come an authoritarian movement, either from the left or from the right and probably from both, which will sap the democratic structure.[4]

3. Fascism a revolt of the lower middle classes. Other observers have tended to accept the view that fascism is the revolt of the lower middle classes. The impoverished but proud rural peasantry, the debt-burdened small landowners, professional workers, struggling shopkeepers and small producers suffering from the competition of large factories and department stores had become disillusioned with capitalism and grown hostile to big business; yet they repudiated the idea of belonging to the proletariat. A political party which was both anti-capitalist and anti-socialist at the same time was particularly appealing to them because it offered the hope of maintaining their superior but sharply challenged status. The socialist and communist parties were unattractive to these groups because they viewed the disappearance of the middle class into the proletariat as an inevitable development. After all, those who don't want to be considered proletariat and who feel oppressed are probably in a majority.

The apprehensions upon which this idea is based are less intense in America than in other countries. In Europe the social pyramid is more sharply defined, and hence the fear of middle class people for their future and their status was much greater because they knew that if they were to sink to the status of manual laborers they could not recover their position.

In Germany there was considerable evidence to substantiate a theory of fascism as the revolt of the lower middle classes; for the Nazis made an earnest effort to appeal to this group and to secure their support. One of the original twenty-five points in the party program demanded "the creation and maintenance of a healthy middle class; the immediate communalization of the big department stores and the lease of the various departments at a low rate to small traders, and that the greatest consideration shall be shown to all small traders supplying goods to the State, the federal states or the municipalities." Another point in the program demanded a thorough

4. See Hans Kelsen, "The Party Dictatorship," *Politica*, II (March, 1936), 19–32; Charles E. Merriam, *The New Democracy and the New Despotism* (New York, 1939), p. 197.

land reform including the expropriation of land for social purposes, the abolition of rent on land, and the prohibition of all speculation in land. Adolf Hitler later explained that this provision was directed primarily against Jewish firms which speculated in land. However, Nazi propaganda continuously extolled the peasant as "the foundation of Germany's future" and promised a "restoration of the remunerative capacity of agriculture." Small peasants, who were heavily in debt but who had no sympathy for the Marxist attitude towards private property, joined the movement because it promised to free them from the burden of interest payments. Undoubtedly the National Socialist opposition to Marxism, its emphasis on nationalism, and its opposition to huge trusts, unearned income, and high interest rates were particularly attractive to lower middle class groups.[5]

SOCIAL COMPOSITION

All of these generalizations are really efforts to explain the rise of fascism; for up to now communist movements have been successful only in peasant countries and not in areas of advanced industrialization. Contrary to Marx's predictions, the middle classes in industrial societies have grown increasingly large and prosperous; an intensification of the class struggle has not accompanied the development of capitalism; the workers in most industrial states today enjoy an increasing standard of living; and the Marxian expectation of increasing misery and increasing exploitation has not been fulfilled. It was in feudalistic Russia where there was no middle class, and not the capitalistic countries of the West, that a communist movement first came to power. In general it may be said that communism has up to now been successful in underdeveloped areas where the masses living in the midst of abject poverty are caught in the dilemma of not being able to survive either in cities that are not industrialized enough to absorb them or in villages that are too overcrowded and poor to yield them a subsistence. Thus peasant discontent, organized under communist leadership and usually transformed into a militant nationalist movement

5. For a discussion of fascism as a middle class movement, see Harold D. Lasswell, "The Psychology of Hitlerism as a Response of the Lower Middle Class to Continuing Insecurity," in his *The Analysis of Political Behavior* (New York, 1948), pp. 235–245; David J. Saposs, "The Role of the Middle Class in Social Development," in *Economic Essays in Honor of Wesley Clair Mitchell* (New York, 1935), pp. 395–424.

directed against the "imperialist" West, has usually been the means by which communism has come to power. Czechoslovakia would seem to provide an exception to this rule, but in this case Russian intervention and the temporary prestige of a "liberating" army, rather than the internal social structure of the country, would seem to account for communist success.[6]

These theories apply to fascism, rather than to dictatorship in general, for another reason. This is because the stage of economic development reached in a given society cannot be considered as the decisive factor in the appearance of dictatorship. For example, tyranny arose in Greek states and medieval cities that had not yet reached the capitalist stage of development. The Spanish colonies in America, which turned to dictatorship as soon as they achieved their independence in the early nineteenth century, were no further advanced in economic organization than the English colonies which revolted in the eighteenth century. Fritz Lehmann in a careful study of the distribution of wealth found that the concentration of economic power was considerably less in Germany than in Great Britain and the United States.[7] As a matter of fact, it is impossible even

6. For an interesting analysis of the conflict between Marxian class theory and the facts of social stratification, see David Mitrany, *Marx Against the Peasant* (Chapel Hill, 1951), especially pp. 205–206: "The startling fact is that Communism has only come to power where by all Marxist tenets it might have been least expected that it could. In every instance, from 1917 in Russia to 1949 in China, Communism has ridden to victory on the back of disaffected peasantries; in no instance has it come near to victory in industrialized 'proletarian' countries. So far it has always been a 'proletarian' revolution without a proletariat; a matter of Communist management of peasant discontent. But while this shows that in the countries where this has happened the peasants were ripe for revolt, it does not show that they inclined to Communism. As regards eastern Europe at any rate, the evidence is all the other way."

7. Fritz Lehmann, "Distribution of Wealth," in Max Ascoli and Fritz Lehmann (eds.), *Political and Economic Democracy* (New York, 1937), pp. 162–163. Professor Lehmann says that in 1930 the wealthiest 2 per cent of the population in the United States owned between 40 and 45 per cent of all private wealth and that "the distribution of wealth in Great Britain appears to be very similar to that in the United States. In Germany, on the other hand, the inequality of property is remarkably less accentuated. In 1927 mark-millionaires possessed hardly more than 3 per cent of all private wealth; those who owned more than 100,000 marks possessed only 10 to 12 per cent of the total. This relatively equal distribution, nevertheless denounced as intolerable by some writers, was not the natural outcome of economic tendencies, nor was it the deliberate effect of an equalitarian policy; it resulted from the postwar inflation. Before the war the millionaires in Prussia owned about 20 per cent and the rich and well-to-do another 25 per cent. Thus while the wealthiest strata possessed almost half of all fortunes before the war and inflation, they owned no more than one-sixth after the catastrophe."

to say that dictatorship results from the efforts of a possessing class to defend itself. Although this explanation covers many examples, it does not account for the revolutionary dictator. It is true that dictatorship has usually been the result of an acute internal conflict in society and that such conflicts have generally had an economic basis. However, these conflicts have arisen during all phases of transition in the economic history of society. The significant question is why have these conflicts occurred in some societies and not in others and why it is that when they arose they became acute in some countries and not in others.

Even if the analysis is limited to Fascism in Italy and Nazism in Germany, it is by no means certain that they were essentially middle class movements. Although party membership is not the same thing as electoral support and although it is a party's supporters, rather than the social composition of its membership, which determines its success, available information indicates that both of these parties drew their members from all strata of the population. In contrast to the socialist and communist parties, which were essentially class parties in the sense that a large majority of their members were manual workers, the fascist parties were quite heterogeneous in their membership, as the following table shows.[8]

These figures compared with those for the population as a whole do show a disproportionate number of party members from middle class groups, but the active members of these parties nevertheless came from many sections of the population whose interests frequently conflicted under ordinary circumstances. It is impossible to account for the success of totalitarian movements by specifying

8. The table is copied from Reinhard Bendix, "Social Stratification and Political Power," *The American Political Science Review*, XLVI (June, 1952), 370. The figures for Germany are taken from H. H. Gerth, "The Nazi Party," *American Journal of Sociology*, XLV (January, 1940), 527, and those for Italy are taken from Herman Finer, *Mussolini's Italy* (New York, 1935), p. 143. Figures on the social composition of the German Communist party are found in Ossip Flechtheim, *Die KPD in der Weimarer Republik* (Offenbach, 1948), p. 236. It is probably impossible at this date to determine with any certainty the social composition of the SPD. However, the Social Democrats were generally recognized as a pro-labor party, enjoyed almost constant success in districts predominantly industrial, and made their appeal to the electorate largely in terms of working-class interests. Sigmund Neumann, *Die deutschen Parteien* (Berlin, 1932), p. 28, says: "It [the SPD] had in its membership in 1930 about 60% workers, 10% employers, 3% civil servants, and 17% housewives." Many authorities are inclined to consider these figures too low so far as working-class support is concerned. However, even if they are accepted, they substantiate the statement made in the text.

PER CENT DISTRIBUTION OF NAZI AND FASCIST PARTY MEMBERS IN DIFFERENT OCCUPATIONS, 1933 (GERMANY) AND 1921 (ITALY)

Nazi Party Members, 1933 (Germany)		Fascist Party Members, 1921 (Italy)	
Manual workers	31.5	Small Traders and Artisans	9.8
White Collar	21.5	Industrialists	3.0
Self Employed	17.6	State Servants (including soldiers and	
Peasants	12.6	civil servants)	5.1
Officials	6.7	Salaried Employees	10.6
Others	10.5	Teachers	1.2
		Students	14.2
		Merchant Marine	1.0
		Industrial Workers	16.5
		Agricultural Workers	26.0
		Landowners (including small proprietors and contractors)	12.8

their sociological makeup before the conquest of power because such a method contributes nothing towards an understanding of the reasons *why* the movement was successful. A totalitarian movement does not conquer a state through the strength of its regular following. "It conquers," as Professor Reinhard Bendix has pointed out, "because some crisis situation adds to that following a significant portion of the electorate as well as the politically indifferent public, whose previous political allegiance or indifference have been transformed rather suddenly by the cumulative pressure of adverse circumstances." [9]

A study of German election statistics shows quite clearly that this was the case. The first major success of the National Socialists occurred in the 1930 elections when there was an eightfold increase in their total vote. In 1928 the party received only 810,127 votes and 12 seats in the Reichstag, but two years later party support had increased to 6,379,672 votes and 107 seats in the Reichstag. [10] A careful study of the probable source of this electoral support provides considerable reason to doubt that National Socialism was essentially a middle class movement. Approximately 2,444,990 persons decided to vote in the 1930 election who had not participated

9. Bendix, *op. cit.*, p. 373.
10. Election statistics can be found in Wilhelm Dittman, *Das Politische Deutschland vor Hitler* (Zurich, 1945).

in the previous election and an additional 1,758,234 young people became eligible and voted for the first time. In this election the Communist party gained 1,325,367 votes, but the only other parties to gain were the small middle class parties and the Catholic Center party which together polled over a million more votes than in 1928. All other parties lost votes, the loss ranging from 270,000 by the Democratic party to almost 2 million by the German Nationalist party. It would appear that this sudden change of the Nazis from an unimportant splinter group to a major contestant for power resulted primarily from the participation of about 4,200,000 nonvoters and young people plus a shift in the allegiance of some voters who had formerly supported the nationalist parties of the Right.

The importance of the previous nonvoters and of the newly eligible young people in this election casts doubt on the conception of fascism as a middle class movement. Although no evidence is available concerning their social composition, there is no reason to believe that they were all, or even predominantly, members of the middle class. In fact, most students of electoral behavior have noticed that political apathy occurs in all strata of a population but that it occurs most frequently among those enjoying the least education and income.[11] On this basis, it would be safe to assume that a greater percentage of those who had refused to vote in previous elections were workers rather than members of the middle class.

It would be incorrect to say that the economic insecurity of middle class groups was not an important factor and that it ought not to be taken into account in explaining the growth of the Nazi party. The elections of 1932 showed a growing support of the Nazis among middle class voters; for in that year the small middle class parties lost 3,740,000 votes as compared with their strength in 1930 and the nationalist parties suffered a further loss of 1.5 million votes. This, together with the addition of 2 million new voters, gave the Nazis 13,765,781 votes and 230 seats in the Reichstag, roughly twice the strength they had had in the previous election. However, it was the nonvoters and the new voters in the 1930 election who provided the original impetus and who transformed the party into

11. See Herbert Tingsten, *Political Behavior* (London, 1937), pp. 120–156, 230.

a mass movement. A major change in the votes of middle class people, and other social groups as well, did not occur until 1932 after the Nazis had already become a major political party and an important contender for power.[12]

It is impossible to suggest here the different motives which influenced people to support the Nazis. Undoubtedly many members of the middle class, and other groups as well, hoped for relief from economic distress. Perhaps others joined in the hope of gaining from backing a victorious movement. The disinterested voters, who normally viewed political participation as "useless" and who usually professed a lack of concern with public affairs, were somehow stimulated to vote for the Nazis and made it into a mass movement. Such people are unlikely to participate in elections except when political tension is high, and they are more likely to vote for a party dedicated to a complete "clean-up" and the establishment of a new order. As a matter of fact, it has been suggested that the survival of democratic institutions does not depend upon a more widespread participation in politics, as is commonly supposed, but that it depends instead upon a fairly persistent residue of political apathy. This is because, in countries such as Germany where the majority of voters are firmly committed to one party or another, the nonparticipants are willing to acquiesce in the democratic process and to ignore its many imperfections. When public interest increases to the point where political participation becomes unusually high, such interest may be the symptom of an intense political controversy which threatens the existence of a democratic system.[13] In order to "explain" the rise of totalitarian movements, it is necessary to know what factors contributed towards the creation of a revolutionary situation. The reasons for the increasing weakness of established institutions is as important as the reasons for the strength of the totalitarian threat. An analysis of the social composition of totali-

12. "If we add all the lost and gained votes for the 1930 and 1932 elections, we find that all the parties between the Nazis and the Communists lost 2,691,688 votes in 1930, but 6,132,692 votes in 1932. Yet the 1930 election had 4,203,224 new voters, while the 1932 election had 1,925,883 new voters. It is apparent that the major increase of Nazi votes came from the new voters in 1930, while the major change in the votes of people in the middle class (and other social groups) occurred in 1932." Bendix, *op. cit.*, p. 370.

13. Tingsten, *op. cit.*, pp. 225–226; Bendix, *op. cit.*, p. 372. In Germany the percentage of voters increased from 75.6 in 1928 to 88.7 in 1933.

tarian movements cannot increase our understanding of these factors because they are likely to be very complex and to vary considerably from country to country.[14]

There is no evidence to support the view that affiliation with, or membership in, a social group engenders a homogeneity of belief which leads to a collective political action. The interests of different classes are not wholly contradictory, and the choice of opposing policies is frequently made on other grounds than those of class. History offers no example of a class dictatorship in the Marxian sense of the word. Soviet Russia is not a dictatorship of the proletariat but the dictatorship of a party, and the so-called "dictatorship of the bourgeoisie" is equally non-existent. The power of the bourgeoisie was never and nowhere greater than in mid-Victorian England; yet this period was the heyday of liberalism when political dictation of all kinds was loathed and when discussion, criticism, and opposition were glorified. "Dictatorship" as applied to classes is nothing more than a propagandistic device meaning paramount influence, and the manner of its use by Marxists leads to an oversimplification of the actual conflict between classes. For example, it is true that the Nazis made a strong appeal to large sections of the middle classes, especially to those who had lost their wealth and positions of social influence during the inflation. But the conflict in Germany must not be viewed in terms of two or three economic classes, each one of which was trying to seize control of the state and use this power to promote its own interests. No modern industrial state can be realistically described in such simple terms. In the case of Germany there were the small peasant proprietors and the greater Junker landlords; there were great industrial magnates and the owners of small retail establishments; and there were, in addition, the great body of workers which consisted of both the skilled and unskilled, organized and unorganized. No two of these many groups were likely to view all political issues alike; a single one of these classes could not possibly win control of the state in a democratic election; and there is no evidence that class

14. Hannah Arendt, *The Origins of Totalitarianism* (New York, 1951), p. 264, says that as political tension increased in Germany and a larger number of people began to demand change at any price the old class lines, which had formed a basis for the party system, became blurred and "class divisions disappeared from the political scene."

solidarity, even in Germany, had reached the point where any one of these groups thought and acted alike.[15]

Governments do not as a rule create the social order which they maintain but are instead a reflection of the existing class structure. To presume that a given institutional system is a gigantic plot whereby the ruling classes maintain themselves in power is to falsify history and oversimplify the facts. A dominant class is interested in far more than its economic interests; it is also concerned with the maintenance of status, with social recognition, and with the power which accompanies its position. If history records a continuous struggle for power and place, it also records that under one set of conditions those in control of property win out but that under another set of conditions they are defeated by the superior organization, the superior numbers, and the superior leadership of their opponents. Although there are frequent clashes for a greater share of and control over the available wealth of the community and although such struggles can alter to some extent the distribution of wealth among the various classes, still the amount each group enjoys is determined primarily by the productivity of the total economy. In the modern world power attaches far more to the management than to the ownership of property, and hence there is a closer resemblance between the power structure of capitalism and of socialism than is commonly supposed.

The rise of totalitarian movements must be studied in terms of the broad cultural and political context of the countries involved. A study of the relationship between social stratification and political action can lead to only tentative conclusions because it is impossible for the analyst to predict what will happen without considering a number of factors, such as local conditions, historical antecedents, the intensity of a totalitarian movement's organiza-

15. R. M. MacIver, *The Web of Government,* p. 91, gives an excellent description of the nature of group conflict in the modern state. He says that "economic power is multi-centered and is the scene of internecine warfare, business against business, industry against industry, capital against labor, industry seeking to cheapen agriculture and *vice versa,* primary producer against manufacturer, manufacturer against retailer, with wholesaler jockeying for position against both, domestic producer against importer, banker against borrower, white collar class squeezed between the demands of other interests, and so on through a multifarious jumble of relationships. Every economic position is relative, every economic gain to one group is a cost from the viewpoint of some other group, and the greater the gain the greater the cost."

tional drive, and the acuteness of the crisis both psychologically and economically. For example, Rudolf Heberle's analysis of party affiliations and their regional differences in the province of Schleswig-Holstein during the Weimar Republic found that in areas of small independent farm holdings a majority of the farmers belonged to the democratic parties and that neither the Social Democrats nor the Communists could make much headway among them.[16] However, French Communists have been successful in their appeals to peasants in areas of small holdings and backward production methods when their German comrades were not.[17] The explanation of this fact obviously involves a broader analysis than a study of social stratification taken alone permits, and it involves the evaluation, as well as the understanding of, a large number of factors and their relationship to one another.

Disintegrating political behavior is not produced by isolated factors, such as the concentration of wealth or power in a minority group, unemployment of a certain size, social discrimination or racial contrasts. In order to understand, it is necessary to study the social structure as a whole and the relationship of each class to the total picture.[18] When unemployment is a familiar experience to a class, it is likely to have a different political effect than when it encroaches upon a class which has rarely known it. The poor are not necessarily repelled by the presence of great wealth but by ideas held concerning its meaning. If it is believed that riches have been laboriously acquired and that they are being wisely spent, the political effect differs from where the opposite view is widely held. Far more important than objective changes of status in the class structure are opinions held concerning their meaning. In other words, it is how social stratification appears to the classes, rather than the sociological facts, which often have political importance. Obviously the chances for error in making an appraisal and the opportunities for a propagandistic misrepresentation of facts are great. The examples given here are intended merely to suggest the

16. Rudolf Heberle, *From Democracy to Nazism* (Baton Rouge, 1945), esp. pp. 90–120.
17. Henry Ehrmann, "The French Peasant and Communism," *American Political Science Review*, XLVI (March, 1952), 19–43.
18. Karl Polanyi, *The Great Transformation* (New York, 1944), p. 152, says: "Neither the birth nor the death of classes, neither their aims nor the degree to which they attain them, neither their co-operations nor their antagonisms can be understood apart from the situation of society as a whole."

scope and complexity of the problem and the elasticity of the method needed for an intelligent study of political action.[19] Those who are content with a slogan or a short and simple answer to explain political happenings need not and ought not to study politics. No class or group is inherently or necessarily anti-democratic. A given political reaction in one country does not necessarily recur under similar economic conditions in another.

THE PROPAGANDA THEORY

To prove their assertion that fascism was a gigantic capitalist plot, Marxian writers are compelled to fall back upon the propaganda theory which asserts that the masses were manipulated by the clever use of propaganda. They are encouraged in this view by many statements made by leading Fascists and Nazis themselves. As is well known, Hitler was particularly interested in propaganda techniques. *Mein Kampf* is largely a treatise on the art of political propaganda; and, along with Dr. Joseph Goebbels, Hitler became the world's foremost exponent of propaganda as a method of controlling opinion. The Nazis carefully employed most of the devices discovered by modern psychology and drew upon the experience made available by modern advertising. Nazi theory proceeded upon the assumption that man is not a rational animal, that he is subject to emotion rather than to reason, that political pronouncements should not be deliberative but present exclusively the idea or view which they are designed to advance, and that propaganda was useful mainly to manipulate opinion and as a weapon in the struggle for power.

From these facts it is easy to draw the conclusion that the Nazis supported by rich financial interests "fooled" the people who were unable to see the impossibility of their promises and that through the clever use of propaganda techniques the masses were persuaded to give their support to a movement inimical to their own interests. However, propaganda does not take place in a vacuum, and it is more than merely a technique for manipulating the masses. It has long been recognized that propaganda can persuade people only to actions that are consonant with their inclinations. Thousands of

19. For a discussion, see Hans Speier, "Social Stratification," in Max Ascoli and Fritz Lehmann (eds.), *Political and Economic Democracy* (New York, 1937), pp. 255–270.

people "hit the sawdust trail" under the spell of an evangelist only to turn their backs on his religion the following day. No matter how skillful an orator may be and no matter how much he plays upon the emotions of his audience, he cannot long maintain his hold unless he evokes convictions and unless he appears to supply a deep-felt need which his listeners harbored consciously or unconsciously long before coming into contact with him. The demagogue cannot create a revolutionary spirit. He may foster it and direct it, but he is likely to be more effective if he is imbued with the doctrine he preaches. Most of the great revolutionary leaders in both religion and politics have been fanatics for the faith. If Lenin and Hitler had been mere technicians of propaganda, mere experts in the manipulation of symbols, mere professionals in exploiting the credulities of their fellows, they would never have moved the world.[20] Although skill in propaganda has become one of the most effective roads to political power, it does not have unlimited possibilities. It is no more miraculous than commercial advertising; and, like other forms of propaganda, depends for its success or failure upon its ability to find a market and to supply a need.

The "propaganda theory" has served a useful purpose by focusing attention upon the fact that man does not always act consciously in the light of reason. Although it had long been known by every successful politician that an emotional appeal is frequently more successful than an appeal to man's intelligence, this fact had been almost completely forgotten or else conveniently overlooked by most democratic theorists. Although furnishing an interesting and important insight into the nature of man, the "propaganda theory" is not a satisfactory explanation for the rise of dictatorship. If we admit that the masses can be lured merely by propaganda, there can be no justification for democracy. Prior to the victory of fascism practically all means of propaganda were in the hands of uncompromising enemies of fascism. The real question is why Nazi and Fascist propaganda were successful in spite of their many contradictions and in spite of vigorous criticisms by the press and radio at the time.

20. R. M. MacIver, *Leviathan and the People* (Baton Rouge, 1939), pp. 133–134; Theodore Abel, *Why Hitler Came to Power* (New York, 1938), pp. 119–120. For a discussion of propaganda in general, see Harwood L. Childs (ed.), *Propaganda and Dictatorship* (Princeton, 1936).

Peter Drucker argues that the people were not fooled by Nazi promises and that they joined the movement, not because they believed in its promises, but because they did not believe in them. He says that nobody would have been a Nazi if rational belief in their promises were a prerequisite, and he gives a number of illustrations from his own experience which show an almost universal disbelief towards Nazi promises and indifference towards the party creed by even the most fanatical Nazis. Moreover, party leaders never pretended to speak the truth. Hitler frankly admitted in *Mein Kampf* that lying is necessary, and Nazi leaders publicly proclaimed their disregard for truth and the impossibility of their promises. Dr. Goebbels is reported to have said in mass meetings, not on one occasion but at several times, when the people cheered a particularly choice lie: "Of course, you understand all this is just propaganda." But the masses only cheered louder!

The masses must have known that Hitler's promises were incompatible each with the other. They may have been taken in in spiritual matters such as the simultaneity of rabid anti-Christian propaganda with equally fervent assertions that Nazism is the savior of the churches. But German farmers trained by a hundred years of co-operative organization, and German workers after sixty years of trade-unionism and collective bargaining, could not have failed to notice the glaring conflict between simultaneous promises—such as, for instance, those made by Dr. Goebbels in one and the same speech in 1932—that the farmer would receive more for his grain, the worker pay less for his bread, and the baker and grocer have a higher wholesale and retail margin. And what about the Berlin metal-workers' strike in 1932—one of the most embittered labor conflicts in German history—when the Nazis together with the Communists supported the strike against the official trade unions who had called it off, while Hitler at the very same moment promised the extremely class-conscious metal manufacturers in a public speech that under Nazism they would again be master in their own house? Result: half the workers and almost all the industrialists turned Nazi. Yet no propaganda could have made employers in the Berlin metal industry or German workers overlook or forget such a contradiction.[21]

What then is the explanation? These astonishing feats were witnessed and commented on by a hostile press, a hostile radio, a hostile church, and a hostile government. It must have been obvious to everyone that the Nazis were inconsistent and that their promises

21. Peter Drucker, *The End of Economic Man* (New York, 1939), pp. 17–18.

were unattainable; yet the masses apparently believed in fascism even though they did not believe its promises.

Although this psychology may appear most extraordinary and complicated, Mr. Drucker finds that it is in fact quite simple. It is the despair of the masses, the tendency often found in ordinary life to believe against belief, the hope for a miracle against all reason and knowledge because the alternative is too terrible to face.

> . . . in despair the masses turned to the magician who promises to make the impossible possible: to make the workers free and simultaneously to make the industrialist "master in his own house"; to increase the price of wheat and at the same time lower the price of bread; to bring peace, yet to bring victory in war; to be everything to everybody and all things to all men. So it is not in spite of but because of its contradictions and its impossibility that the masses turn to fascism. For if you are caught between the flood of the past, through which you cannot retrace your steps, and an apparently unscalable blank wall in front of you, it is only by magic and miracles that you can hope to escape. . . .
>
> The despair of the masses is the key to the understanding of fascism. No "revolt of the mob," no "triumphs of unscrupulous propaganda," but stark despair caused by the breakdown of the old order and the absence of a new one.[22]

FINANCIAL SUPPORT

Those who believe that fascism was a capitalist plot have generally offered little proof beyond the reconstruction of political events in terms of their own bias and the assertion that since the movement did not serve the best interests of workers it must have had a pro-capitalist motive. Obviously such writers presuppose the very thing that they are trying to prove. Even if it is admitted that the measures undertaken by Fascists and National Socialists after they came to power benefited the "economic royalists," this fact, and it is very debatable as to whether this was actually the case, does not explain their ability to win mass support in the first place nor does it prove the existence of a plot. The most that could be said is that the big industrialists, bankers, and large landowners were able to influence the government and control its policies or that they captured control of the movement after it came to power.

Documentary proof of the assertion that fascism was a capitalist plot is scanty, and reliance has been placed primarily upon the fact

22. *Ibid.,* p. 22.

that some industrialists and bankers were among the contributors to party campaign funds. From these facts it has been deduced that the support of rich financial interests was a decisive factor, that business and financial support made it possible to build a superior organization, and that the use of tremendous sums of money not available to other parties made it possible to build a mass movement. The rich magnates could control the movement because they owned it, and if they had not received assurances and guarantees from the party leaders, they would not have furnished the money. These ideas are plausible enough and they merit careful consideration.

It is always difficult to secure reliable information about party finances, but it is particularly difficult for Germany and Italy because there were no laws limiting the amount of money to be spent in elections or requiring the publication of campaign funds. A party cannot build an organization and carry on propaganda activities without the expenditure of funds; and if it is a large national party appealing to many different groups and interests, the expenditure of large sums is obviously necessary. Although Hitler had contacted several leaders of industry and finance as early as 1927 and gained the support of some, such as Fritz Thyssen and Emil Kirdoff, there is no evidence that the rich financial magnates generally supported the movement. As a matter of fact, a main source of income appears to have been the dues and contributions received from rank-and-file party members and collections taken up at party meetings. Frequently a fee was charged for admission to campaign meetings, a practice which was followed by the Social Democrats and other parties as well; and during the second electoral campaign of 1932 uniformed agents of the Nazis solicited contributions on the streets of large cities. Practically all accounts agree that Nazi finances were often stringent. Theodore Abel in his study, based upon the biographies of 600 party members, records that local leaders enjoying only a modest income frequently paid expenses out of their own pockets.[23]

In so far as total party expenditures are concerned, the opinion of the best authority on the subject is that the Social Democratic party spent for both national and local purposes in 1930 nearly fifteen million marks. The yearly expenditures of the Nationalists

23. Abel, *op. cit.*, pp. 90–91.

were estimated at six or seven million marks, the National Socialists at five million, the Center party a million and a half, the Democratic or State party about a million, and the Communists also at about a million marks.[24] If superior funds for organization, propaganda, and electioneering purposes were a decisive factor, the Social Democrats, who had the most money and whose funds were derived almost entirely from small weekly contributions, or dues, from party members, should have been able to prevent Nazi success. The Nationalists also spent more money, yet they continued to lose supporters to the growing Nazi movement. Both the Nationalist and People's parties had a greater number of well-to-do members able to make large donations. In Germany contributions were made not only by individuals but also by large businesses, banks, and other corporate interests. Although it would be inaccurate to say that business, either large or small, supported any single political party, the Nationalist party probably received more business support than any other group. As a matter of fact, many large corporate interests simultaneously contributed to two, three, or more political parties in the hope of spreading good will and encouraging candidates friendly to their interests. It is easier for a party to secure financial support when there is a prospect for success; for many like to be on the winning side and believe it good business to have contributed to the party's victory. As Nazi strength increased, so did the financial aid given by German capital; but these funds were attracted by success after the Nazis had already become an important political movement.[25] Hence it cannot be argued that Hitler's successes were the result of enormous financial aid given by big industrial and financial interests in accordance with a preconceived plan for establishing a popular movement capable of preventing the rise of socialism.

24. J. K. Pollock, *Money and Politics Abroad* (New York, 1932), pp. 214–215. See also Fritz Thyssen, *I Paid Hitler* (New York, 1941), pp. 97–105; Frederick L. Schuman, *The Nazi Dictatorship* (New York, 1935), pp. 85–94; Konrad Heiden, *Der Fuehrer* (Boston, 1944), pp. 339–343.

25. Fritz Thyssen, *op. cit.,* pp. 102–103, says: "It was during the last years preceding the Nazi seizure of power that the big industrial corporations began to make their contributions. But they did not give directly to Hitler; they gave it to Dr. Alfred Hugenberg, who placed about one-fifth of the donated amounts at the disposal of the National Socialist party. . . . But Hitler's relations did not extend to industrialists in general. In fact, besides old Kirdoff, who was not really an owner of heavy industrial works, I was the only one of that ilk who freely exposed himself in this connection."

Italy presented a similar situation. The main body of the
bourgeoisie apparently regarded Mussolini as an adventurer and
was suspicious of his socialist background. Some industrialists and
large landowners supported the Fascists as a sort of militia to aid in
breaking troublesome strikes and in combatting socialist violence.
However, not all of even these individuals were enthusiastic about
a Fascist government. Many belonged to other parties and thus had
their party in Parliament and regarded the Fascists merely as an
extra insurance to take direct action in the streets. At the time of
the march on Rome there were still only 35 Fascist deputies in
Parliament out of a total membership of 535. Mussolini was successful very largely because the government was weak and vacillat-
ing, because it could not restore order and protect individual
rights, and because the opposition was hopelessly divided and poorly
led. As one outstanding authority has said, the Fascists were "the
one wilful, ruthless force, determined to achieve their object." [26]
The fact that certain individuals contributed to Fascist party funds
does not in itself prove that it was a capitalist party any more than
the fact that most Bolshevist leaders were of middle class origin
proves that communism is a movement devoted to the protection
of middle class interests.

APPEAL TO ALL GROUPS

Fascism was essentially a popular movement which appealed to
all groups and classes. Although a greater percentage of certain
social groups were perhaps more disposed to join the movement,
an attempt was made in both Germany and Italy to enlist the support of all groups and classes. The fact that this effort was somewhat successful accounts for the importance fascism achieved in
these two countries. In 1921 more than 50 per cent of the membership of the Fascist party was working-class, and in Germany the
National Socialist party also had a large working-class element.

Although social conflict has frequently accompanied the rise of
dictatorship, it is difficult to understand why, according to Marxian
theory, the only conflict that has any importance is the conflict
between the two classes into which the modern world is supposedly
divided. There was no social conflict in Turkey or Poland.[27] In

26. Finer, *Mussolini's Italy,* p. 145.
27. "In Poland neither Socialism nor Communism played much part in the

Yugoslavia the source of the antagonism which made dictatorship possible lay in geographical and local, rather than class, hostility. In Germany the Nazis established an anti-communist dictatorship, but there was no danger of a communist revolution prior to their seizure of power. Even in Italy there was no capitalist organization to intervene when the workers seized control of the factories in 1920. It is generally agreed that the socialist movement had failed before the Fascists became powerful and that the fascist movement did not, as according to communist theory it should have, step in and seize the prize from the workers when they were on the point of gaining it.

It cannot, however, be denied that economic distress and the intensification of class bitterness have played an important role in the rise of dictatorships. It is equally true that fear drove many a capitalist to fascist defenses. However, the fascist type of dictatorship cannot be understood in terms of these isolated factors but only as a response to the whole tangled situation. As Lord Bryce pointed out, it is facts that are needed. "When facts have been supplied each of us can try to reason from them." [28] Today the very opposite method is often used. A theory is supplied and facts are presented to document or reinforce preconceived assumptions.

Karl Marx directed his attack against both nationalism and capitalism, and for the purposes of his polemic identified the two principles. In the pursuit of his aim to overthrow both of them together he simplified and exaggerated the role of class distinctions. He defined social class in purely economic terms and concluded that each of the two classes so distinguished had a clear-cut difference in outlook, morals, interest, and philosophy of life. In his philosophy the whole area of common interests was destroyed; and the dividing interests of the farmer and the business man, the small capitalist and the large capitalist, the professional worker and the entrepre-

---

inefficiency which led to the *coup d'état* of 1926. The real Socialist Party was not particularly strong and certainly was not a serious menace to established order; the Communist Party was non-existent. No party was proposing any large transfer of power or property. Pilsudski drew adherents from every class. He was supported by the urban working class, and the railway strike in his support was the decisive factor in his success. The proximity of Russia undoubtedly led people to believe in the necessity of strong government, but it was Russia in her aspect of national State, not of Communist missionary, which Poland feared." Spearman, *Modern Dictatorship*, p. 67.

28. *Modern Democracies* (New York, 1924), I, 12.

neur, the skilled laborer and the unskilled laborer, the importer and the exporter, the industrialist and the financier, and the unorganized white-collar worker and the organized laborer were either minimized or conveniently ignored. The Marxian theory of unmitigated antagonism between two social classes consisting of the expropriators and the expropriated, is not based upon an observation of the facts but on the belief in a socialist state.

The greatest danger inherent in Marxian theory is not its oversimplification of the class struggle but its attitude of intolerance and uncompromising intransigence. If the isolation of classes into separate parties is pushed to its logical conclusion, government by discussion becomes impossible; and irreconcilables face each other across an abyss of divergent interests. Obviously the only means of resisting a party determined on attempting a *coup d'état* is by force, and the use of force will eventually destroy democratic government. When Marxian socialism effectively enters the arena of opinion, it tends to reduce all other opinions to the contrary extreme in order to crush them all. It thus breeds the opposite extreme and precipitates a civil war of opinion. Under these circumstances any middle ground becomes untenable and the country is plunged into civil war until one extreme destroys the other. In Spain absolutist rule and continued suppression tended to breed intransigent radical movements of syndicalism, anarchism, and communism. When in 1931 a republican constitution was adopted, the left came to power and made sweeping demands which might not have been unreasonable under other circumstances but which were extremely premature in view of the lack of preparation for them. Spain failed to build up strong center parties capable of holding the balance between right and left, and hence there was no group to mediate between the two extremes. Under these circumstances there was no prospect for democracy. Instead the issue was whether Spain would be governed by a dictatorship from the left or from the right, and the country was plunged into a bloody civil war to find the answer.[29]

The threat of communist violence is, therefore, one of the chief factors responsible for the rise of dictatorship. It ought not to be forgotten that in Italy the socialists were the first to use force. Although the Communists in Germany did not try violence and war,

29. Frank Manuel, *The Politics of Modern Spain* (New York, 1938).

they never ceased to preach the necessity of a violent revolution. As one author has said, "It seems foolish to complain if the more timid bourgeois thought they really meant what they said." [30]

Opinion is divided concerning which class benefits from fascism. Some writers believe that it is a government of big capitalists; others point out that it attempted to solve the problem of unemployment and conciliate working-class opinion and that it was in many ways solicitous of the welfare of workers; still others see it as a reaction of the lower middle class. The truth of the matter is that both the Nazi and Fascist dictatorships were exercised theoretically in what was conceived to be the national interest, and the special interests of all or any class were sacrificed to this conception. Both governments were extremely critical of capitalism, and their economic policies were not designed to save or restore capitalism. High taxation, the strict control of private investment, an intolerable amount of regulation, supervision, and control of business, and the pressure put on employers to take on more workmen or refrain from dismissing laborers regardless of the needs of the business, and the regulation of profits are only a few characteristics of the policies pursued in both countries which do not appear to fit the capitalist interest. Professor Wilhelm Röpke thinks that the distinguishing characteristic of the Nazi dictatorship was its complete separation from any class.[31] Neither Mussolini nor Hitler ever hesitated to sacrifice any group or interest if they thought it necessary to do so. Practically the only class which directly benefited were the party members. The whole effort to determine which class benefited more than others is, of course, tied in with the Marxian idea that every state has a class basis, and it ignores the fact that all governments are not equally concerned about individual or group welfare and that some governments may be devoted to the national interest as they conceive it without any thought of the economic effect of their policies upon particular groups or classes. Nothing but a dogmatic political faith compels an insistence upon the idea that people are waging the class war even when they claim that they are doing something else.

30. Spearman, *op. cit.,* p. 73.
31. Wilhelm Röpke, "Fascist Economics," *Economica,* II (February, 1935), 85–100; Frieda Wunderlich, "Germany's Defense Economy and the Decay of Capitalism," *Quarterly Journal of Economics,* LII (May, 1938), 401–430.

The Nature of Modern Society

ALTHOUGH it has been fashionable in recent years to speak of dictatorship as an incomprehensible freak and as a reaction against the whole trend of western civilization, conditions inherent in the very nature of modern industrial society pose new problems and help explain the contemporary crisis of democracy. In many countries dictatorship has emerged after the breakdown of established institutions. In other countries it represents a protest against what has become a questionable economic system, a shattered social order, or the injustice of the preceding system. Thus dictatorship has grown out of democracy, is not completely divorced from the past, and is a reaction to modern conditions. The question arises as to what factors inherent in the nature of modern society have contributed to the decline of democracy and the establishment of dictatorship.

Isolation of the Individual

The rise of capitalism destroyed the old medieval social system together with the stability and relative security it offered. Although the individual was freed from the authority of the medieval church and the absolutist state, he was also uprooted with a consequent feeling of insecurity and reduced to becoming a mere cog in a vast machine. Modern man is unable to make decisions affecting the most important aspects of his life, and his feeling of isolation and powerlessness are enhanced by the fear of mass unemployment and the threat of war.

Everywhere he goes and in everything he does he comes into contact with vast impersonal forces. Although he lives in a large city together with thousands of others, he is not integrated into the community and has a terrible feeling of frustration and isolation. At his job he is merely a small part of a vast operation. When he goes to the department store, no one is particularly happy because he came. The clerks who wait on him are employees of a large concern; and, unlike the proprietor of a small store, they do not care whether he buys anything or not. If he joins a trade union to further his economic interests, the union is also likely to be a huge organization in which he cannot play an important role. The individual, therefore, stands alone, confused, frustrated, and over-awed by a consciousness of his lack of importance and powerlessness.

Erich Fromm has shown how every aspect of modern life is calculated to produce a sense of insecurity, doubt, aloneness, and anxiety and that such feelings exist among all classes. The paradox of contemporary society is that "as man becomes more independent, self-reliant and critical he becomes more isolated, alone and afraid" and hence more susceptible to "any custom and any belief, however absurd and degrading, if it only connects the individual with others." Dr. Fromm says that the appeal of fascism can be partially explained by the desire to "escape into submission" from the heavy burden and strain of freedom; for "if we do not see the unconscious suffering of the average atomized person, then we fail to see the danger that threatens our culture from its human basis: the readiness to accept any ideology and any leader, if only he promises excitement and offers a political structure and symbols which allegedly give meaning and order to an individual's life. The despair of the human automaton is fertile soil for the political purposes of Fascism." [1]

It has sometimes been said that men everywhere are desirous of freedom, but an unemotional investigation would subject this statement to considerable doubt. There is, to be sure, the desire for a negative freedom: to be rid of certain oppressions, such as colonial administrators or domestic secret-police forces; but the positive desire to govern oneself and to make constant decisions on matters of public concern is not too widespread in the world. As soon as

1. *Escape from Freedom* (New York, 1941), p. 256.

certain grievances have been eliminated, many people are content to leave the government in the hands of "those who know best."

INCREASED BURDEN ON THE ELECTORATE

Democratic theory assumes that the intellectual qualities of the people are such that they can judge effectively the general quality of the men who seek their votes. Historical experience seems to confirm that the electorate can give a great and simple answer to a great and simple question; but in modern society the number of policies requiring electoral decision have been vastly increased and their nature has become progressively complicated. Hence it has become increasingly difficult to interpret the meaning of election results. One has only to sample the literature on the British election of 1945 or the American Presidential election of 1952 to see how many factors play a role and how difficult it is to say precisely what it was that "the people" thought about the matters discussed in the campaign. In a sense this has always been true. Opinions seldom carry weight in pure proportion to their intrinsic merit. The average man has always made his decision on the basis of a general impression; and trivial matters, rather than important questions of principle, have always influenced his vote. Nevertheless it is far more difficult today to say definitely that an election decides anything other than the personnel of key office holders; and in a multi-party country, such as France, it cannot be said that even this issue is decided by an election. The average man is likely to think that parties exist not because there are two sides to every question but because there are two sides to a political office—an inside and an outside; and he is also likely to feel that it is impossible for him to exert an effective influence on the policies of the government.

GROWTH OF BUREAUCRACY

The assumption of new functions by the state has resulted in the growth of a vast and complicated administrative machine. To deplore and denounce this development is futile; for the economic functions of the modern state cannot be abandoned, have been dictated by public opinion, and have come into being in all modern states as a response to real problems. On the other hand, it is equally ridiculous to ignore this new expansion of administration and argue, as many people do, that because it is necessary, no problem exists.

The increasing complexity of the economic system, the growth of public regulation, the nationalization of industry, and an increasing demand for all kinds of social services have produced a mighty bureaucracy which is highly specialized and which has had professional training in administration. Gone are the days when, as President Jackson said, a government job was either so simple or could be made so simple that the average man could perform it satisfactorily. As administration becomes more and more a closed profession and as the power of this group increases, the ordinary voter is less likely to feel that he lives under a system which makes him one of the governors as well as one of the governed.

The danger of crushing liberty in the name of security has frequently been pointed out; and Professor Mark M. Heald has recently called attention to the fact that as new limitations upon personal freedom are imposed, "no matter how sincere and important the purpose of those restraints, they tend almost automatically to require still further curbs in order to secure the enforcement of the initial restrictions." [2] The more complex the administrative structure becomes, "the greater the need for authority on top and of discipline below. And the greater, consequently, the relative advantages of autocracy and the more baffling the difficulties confronting democracy." [3]

Red tape and bureaucratic inefficiency are problems facing all modern governments—democratic and dictatorial as well. A study of the speeches and of the changes made in party rules at the Nineteenth Communist Party Congress held shortly before Premier Stalin's death confirms that most of the evils ordinarily associated with bureaucracy were a matter of chief concern. [4] However, in a democracy there is the added problem of how to keep this huge administration responsible and sensitive to public opinion. Even in Britain this is today a matter of chief concern. It is generally ad-

2. *A Free Society: An Evaluation of Contemporary Democracy* (New York, 1953), p. 437.

3. William E. Rappard, *The Crisis of Democracy* (Chicago, 1938), p. 262. See also Charles S. Hyneman, *Bureaucracy in a Democracy* (New York, 1950); John D. Kingsley, *Representative Bureaucracy: An Interpretation of the British Civil Service* (Yellow Springs, Ohio, 1944); Paul Appleby, *Big Democracy* (New York, 1945).

4. Harry Schwartz, "Anatomy of the Russian Communist Party," *New York Times Magazine* (March 22, 1953), p. 12; Merle Fainsod, *How Russia Is Ruled* (Cambridge, Mass., 1953), pp. 327–353; Victor Kravchenko, *I Chose Freedom* (New York, 1946), esp. pp. 316–331.

mitted that ministers are more dependent on their permanent civil servants than at any previous time, that ministers probably have little knowledge of what is done in their names or under their nominal responsibility, and that the traditional methods for controlling the administration are far from satisfactory. Members of the House of Commons are finding it increasingly difficult to discuss intelligently much of the highly technical legislation which they are called upon to pass, and they are finding the traditional methods of control over the processes of administration increasingly unsatisfactory.

Up to now the British people have done little more than define "the general aims or objectives" in finding a solution for the administration of nationalized industries. There should be decentralization in order to avoid political pressure and the concentration of too much power at the center. Ministers are responsible to Parliament and must answer questions concerning "the general policy" of each public corporation; but they are not responsible to Parliament and need not answer questions on "the detailed operations," which is the responsibility of a board appointed to manage each public corporation. The workers and other interested groups are represented in "advisory councils" which can influence policy, but the theory of the British constitution which requires "responsibility" to Parliament has been preserved. As might be expected, there has been some disagreement as to whether a given question concerns "general policy" or "detailed operations." General dissatisfaction prompted the appointment of a select committee to study the matter but the issue is far from resolved.[5] Partially because of a general feeling that more time is needed to work out these and other problems of administration, the Labor party has recently announced that no new industries are to be nationalized in the immediate future.

When one contemplates the size and complexity of the governmental machine in any modern state, it is indeed a tribute to the political capacity of the people if the government can be operated at all within a democratic framework. It is impossible to go on

5. W. A. Robson (ed.), *Problems of Nationalized Industry* (London, 1952); articles by D. N. Chester, W. A. Robson, Ernest Davies, G. D. H. Cole, J. A. G. Griffith, et al., in *The Political Quarterly* (April–June, 1950); D. N. Chester, *The Nationalized Industries: An Analysis of the Statutory Provisions* (Second edition; London, 1951).

forever piling bureau upon bureau and constantly increasing the number of boards. The individual citizen will become lost in a maze! Yet a way must be found to restore the idea that he is one of the governors as well as one of the governed. It has been suggested that this can perhaps best be done by creating an opportunity for him to participate, at least to some extent, in the decisions of bodies which most intimately affect his daily life. It is no longer a question as to whether "big government" is a good thing; for the welfare state and its bureaucratic machine are already here. It is instead a question as to whether new administrative techniques can be developed rapidly enough to meet the challenge of the social service state.

GROWTH OF ORGANIZED ECONOMIC POWER

Since the individual standing alone can accomplish nothing, he joins an association to further his interests. Today there are trade unions, employers' organizations, professional societies, agricultural associations, and many other special interest groups. "If we wish to get a correct picture of the social and economic structure of the modern world," Professor E. H. Carr tells us,

> we must think not of a number of individuals cooperating and competing within the framework of a state, but of a number of large and powerful groups, sometimes competing, sometimes cooperating, in the pursuit of their group interests, and of a state constantly impelled to increase the strength and scope of its authority in order to maintain the necessary minimum of cohesion in the social fabric. We can no longer base our thinking, like the classical economists, on the isolated independent individual. The subject of modern economics is man in society, man as a member of a number of collective groups struggling for power, of which the most powerful, the most highly organised and the most broadly based is the state.[6]

The existence of these many groups increases the opportunity for participation by the citizen, but it also raises the question as to what their relationships should be to society as a whole and how these various organizations are to be integrated into community life.

To vast numbers of people political rights have lost their former importance because of the feeling that the unorganized majority of

6. *Conditions of Peace* (New York, 1943), pp. 74–75.

the electorate can accomplish nothing against the overriding force of organized economic power. Even in Great Britain the opinion is growing that politics consist of a bargaining process between the forces representing organized capital and organized labor. It would be an exaggeration to say that the Conservative and Labor parties are nothing more than two machines representing respectively the combined forces of organized capital and organized labor, for electoral considerations compel both major parties to broaden their appeal to include a great deal more than a narrow special group interest. Yet there is considerable evidence to substantiate the charge that political policies are influenced in a major degree by the vested interests who supply the bulk of party funds and only to a minor degree by the opinions of the electorate whom they claim to represent. The domination of economic interest has been furthered by the expense of modern elections and the centralized control of party funds, by the power of the central party machine to influence the selection of candidates, and by the strict control over members of the House of Commons exercised by the party whip. Professor E. H. Carr says that in 1935

> a majority of voters, a majority of members of Parliament and even a majority of the Conservative Party would, on a free and secret vote, have endorsed the report of a Royal Commission which had by a majority advised the withdrawal of the sugar beet subsidy. The economic power of the agricultural interest speaking through the Conservative Party machine prevented the question coming up for a vote and, had a vote been taken, would have been strong enough to secure its rejection.[7]

Undoubtedly a large number of similar illustrations could be given from recent British politics, and instances of this kind help explain why it is that even in Great Britain political rights do not enjoy the prestige they formerly had. Although politicians and political thinkers have denounced the wickedness of gangsters and fascists, the masses have been slow to rally to a defense of political rights because it is widely believed that they no longer confer an effective control over the decisive issues of national life. This attitude was particularly widespread in Weimar Germany where there was a tendency for every special interest group to form itself into a party. Under these circumstances political democracy appeared

7. Carr, *op. cit.,* p. 27.

to be nothing more than the rule of selfish organized interest groups which were antagonistic to one another and which tended to destroy the community.

Under modern conditions it is more difficult to preserve a sense of community because the individual instead of becoming a civic-minded person is likely to be the supporter of a special interest group. Thus what was formerly a uniform and homogeneous opinion under simpler conditions may become broken up into a number of highly specialized functional organizations. Perhaps the flattest denial of the existence of a general political consciousness may be found in the suggestion that the traditional method of basing representation upon territorial constituencies be replaced by a system of functional representation based upon occupational groupings.[8] It is argued that there is no longer any real community of feeling or will in territorial constituencies, that although people live in the same neighborhood they have little in common and pursue very different interests, and that it is no longer possible for a single representative to represent satisfactorily the viewpoint of people assembled in a large city.

There is good reason to doubt whether any real democratic representation can be achieved by grouping people on the basis of their economic or occupational position. This is because vocational interest is not the only and frequently not even the most important determinant of social alignment, because it is difficult to define the groups and distribute representation properly,[9] because representatives from interest groups would be more uncompromising than politicians elected in geographic constituencies, and because such a legislature would be less likely to have a majority behind any positive proposal. If it is suggested that there be two chambers of the legislature, one political and the other economic, then the question arises as to whether they could really be coordinate bodies or whether one chamber would have to be dominant over the other.

8. For a discussion, see G. D. H. Cole, *Social Theory* (London, 1920) and *Guild Socialism Restated* (London, 1920); Sidney Webb, *A Constitution for the Socialist Commonwealth of Great Britain* (London, 1920); F. W. Coker, *Recent Political Thought* (New York, 1934), pp. 261–285.

9. This almost certainly could not be done by voluntary agreement, for each industry, occupation, or profession would regard itself as socially and economically important beyond its numbers and insist upon representation in accordance with its supposed importance to society.

In any case, functional representation has never been used for the choice of bodies having real powers of decision. In both France and Weimar Germany economic councils have served as advisory or consultative bodies, and in Fascist Italy and Salazar's Portugal they have operated under dictatorial conditions. Corporativism has been a technique of dictatorship, rather than an instrument of constitutionality, because a chamber representing different interests can possess no inherent cohesion and because any unity of action which it may attain is likely to be an imposed unity. Occupational representation is a divisive rather than an integrating element because it treats men on the basis of how they are different rather than on the basis of how they are alike. As Herman Finer has pointed out,

> If the principle of government by consent of the governed is accepted, and if that consent is admitted to be shown in free elections, then the integrating will of the nation so emerges from election. If an integrated will is desired, it is most likely to be achieved on a territorial basis in which each electoral district assembles the voters, who are on principle regarded as equal. This is, at any rate, the principle which divides citizens from each other least; and indeed, it can be argued that its appeal to equality and its frown on personal and social and economic differentiae of any kind encourages solidarity.[10]

It is easy to overemphasize the importance of special interest groups. After all, "the" farmer and "the" worker do not replace "the" citizen who as a common man has a mind of his own independent of the groups to which he may belong and who makes decisions and holds opinions about matters of common concern which have no relevance to his occupational interests. There are political issues which transcend in importance a decision based upon a narrow economic self-interest, and history records many instances when the electorate has been moved by an appeal of this kind. On the other hand, it has taken a long time to develop an underlying sense of community and modern conditions introduce a number of divisive factors which make its preservation infinitely more difficult

10. *Theory and Practice of Modern Government* (revised edition; New York, 1949), pp. 544. See also Paul Vignaux, "Corporativism in Europe," *The Review of Politics*, IV (April and July, 1942), 194–205, 303–314; and F. A. Hermens, "Functional Autonomy After World War II," in Arnold J. Zurcher (ed.), *Constitutions and Constitutional Trends Since World War II* (New York, 1951), pp. 116–133.

today. Both fascism and communism have attracted many of their supporters by offering a new sense of the common good shared by all members of the community and by advocating the creation of a new community representing not the victory of one interest over another but the devotion of each person to the common good. They both attempt to secure the union of their supporters by making a conscious plan for the common advantage of the whole community. It is probably true, as the totalitarians contend, that only a few have a genuine sense of the whole community and that democratic theorists have erred in supposing that there is an equal appreciation of the common good among all citizens; but it would appear that the remedy is to educate better citizens rather than to destroy the element of choice and to have each man's good chosen for him.

Exercise of Dictatorial Power Easier

If the nature of modern society has made the emergence of dictatorship psychologically possible, it has also made the exercise of autocratic power easier than in any preceding period. The telephone, telegraph, railways, motor cars, aeroplanes, and other means of transportation and communication make it possible for governments to regulate and control vast areas and huge populations. The military weapons used by a modern army, such as tanks and machine guns, make it possible for a small number of men to dominate a huge population. Gone are the days when an aroused citizenry can take to the streets and overthrow a government which still has the support of the army. The growth of large-scale business organizations has also facilitated centralized governmental control, for it is easier for the state to regulate a small number of huge corporations than to check on a large number of small business men. The emphasis placed upon "scientific management" in modern industry and the development of a huge business bureaucracy have meant that the responsibility for making key decisions has become progressively centered in fewer and fewer hands and that the average person becomes increasingly accustomed to being led by others and gives up his own interpretation of events for those which others give him. The nationalization of industry offers no solution to this problem because in any highly industrial society men are bound to be part of a highly disciplined and authoritative organization. Thus "a modern industrial democratic state has been a house divided against itself, an autocratically governed industry over against a political democracy." [11]

*   *   *   *   *   *

It is impossible to discuss here all the changes brought about by the Industrial Revolution and their psychological effects, but it is easy to see that the cumulative result may be inimical to democracy. Having witnessed how science has conquered terrible diseases, how transportation advances and construction marvels have overcome the former impediments of both distance and space, and how government itself has performed functions previously considered impossible, people no longer feel that the insecurity they experience or the disasters they fear are due to the uncontrollable forces of nature. They are instead inclined to believe that the government can do anything. Such an attitude is fertile ground for the demagogue because the people are credulous and are not likely to detect that he promises more than he can deliver. Moreover, the electorate is likely to be too impatient because it believes all problems are capable of solution and because it is likely to feel that hardships and inconveniences are due to the greed, selfishness, or incompetence of other men or else to the inadequacies of the economic and political system. Thus the emotionally charged propaganda of the demagogue claiming that a particular group is selfishly causing the trouble and ought to be brought under control has a powerful effect.[12] The spread of industry has brought a higher standard of living together with the increase and diffusion of knowledge, but it may in the long run have the effect of discouraging democratic institutions. As a matter of fact, both fascism and communism are so closely connected with contemporary sociological and psychological conditions that they could hardly have come at any other time.

11. A. D. Lindsay, *The Modern Democratic State* (New York, 1943), pp. 186–187. See also Karl Mannheim, *Man and Society in an Age of Reconstruction* (New York, 1941).

12. For example, the Nazis focused their attention on the Jews, the Communists on the capitalists.

The Psychology
of Dictatorship

A complete analysis of political forces must include not only sociological facts but their relationship to opinion. Although there is always an economic and social aspect to political activity, politics has its roots in psychology. A study of symbols and myths may contribute as much to our knowledge of political institutions as a study of the historical background, economic institutions, and the environmental setting. In any case, there is always the human element which must be understood in assessing political movements. In recent years a number of observers, employing a socio-psychological approach, have deduced interpretations of the nature of man and his reactions to contemporary conditions which help explain the popularity of dictatorships. Others, applying mainly psychoanalytical concepts and theories, have attempted the more ambitious task of combining the study of culture and personality so as to provide an integrated approach to the more complex problems of personality, conduct, and social life. The utility of these studies is still a matter of controversy; but their overall effect has been to produce new insights and a better understanding of the nature of modern dictatorship.

Charismatic Leadership

Our age is characterized by a new vogue in personal leadership. In all countries governed by dictators there is a cult of the all-wise ruler who is thought of as the expression and personification of the age and as a man possessing capacities of a higher order than those of ordinary mortals. Max Weber has described such leadership as "charismatic" to indicate the emotional feeling of personal loyalty upon which it is based.[1] Although originally a religious idea meaning literally a "gift of grace" and indicating that the man endowed with charisma is the mouthpiece of God and does the will of God, Max Weber gave it a secular twist to denote those men who, on the basis of personal heroism, magnetism, or other distinctive qualities, are immediately and unqualifiedly recognized by the masses as a leader. The authority of such men is personal rather than traditional and its source is "magical" rather than rational.

Leadership has always been a great factor in the history of human communities. Carlyle, Maurras, Nietzsche, and Leopold von Ranke saw history as largely the work of great state builders. This view has today been generally discredited, and economic determinism has proceeded to interpret the leader as nothing but the product of favorable economic circumstance. Although it is generally agreed that the qualities needed depend upon the conditions under which leadership operates, the nature of the group, and the character of the task to be performed, still it would be an exaggeration to say that it is "the times which make the man." History records many periods in which nations were faced by a severe crisis but intelligent and effective leadership was not forthcoming. Recent studies have centered their attention on the psychological processes associated with leadership and the psychic impulses generated in men by a feeling of insecurity; and although these studies have produced a number of new insights, we are still unable to "explain" leadership and probably always will be.[2]

Although charismatic rule has long been neglected and ridiculed, it is a recurring idea in history. King Saul of Israel was anointed by Samuel, the prophet of God. Deification of the ruler characterized the oriental monarchies, and the idea was imported

1. See H. H. Gerth and C. Wright Mills (translators and editors), *From Max Weber: Essays in Sociology* (New York, 1946), pp. 245–252 and A. M. Henderson and Talcott Parsons (translators and editors), *Max Weber: Theory of Social and Economic Organization* (New York, 1947), pp. 358–392.

2. For an incisive study, see Sidney Hook, *The Hero in History, A Study in Limitation and Possibility* (New York, 1943).

into Europe by King Alexander of Macedonia. The Hellenistic monarchies, which followed, were partially held together by the belief that the king was himself a god; and the deification of Roman Emperors, who inherited this tradition, is familiar to every student of history. At the beginning of bourgeois society the rising middle classes, who had great need for peace and tranquillity, endowed the king with superhuman qualities and invoked the authority of the Scriptures as well as Lutheran and Calvinist teachings in support of absolute monarchy. It would appear, therefore, that the leader's charismatic power is not a mere phantasy, that it has deep roots, and that it becomes a powerful stimulus once the proper psychological and social conditions are set.

Charisma is an irrational belief which arises in situations which the average man cannot grasp and understand rationally. In periods of civil strife, religious turmoil, and profound social and economic upheavals, men are often unable to perceive the factors which have caused their misery and distress. Under such circumstances they are likely to look for a leader who will fend off misery and deliver them from destitution. An examination of the idolatrous utterances made by party members, university professors, army officers, business men, and ordinary workers indicates quite clearly that contemporary leaders are revered and that they are thought of as possessing qualities lacking in ordinary mortals. In Nazi Germany hero-worship was formulated into a definite theory, for there were "Führers" for every branch of activity. However, Hermann Goering's description in *Germany Reborn* is similar to the adoration of the person of the dictator in other countries:

> Just as the Roman Catholic considers the Pope infallible in all matters concerning religion and morals, so do we National Socialists believe, with the same inner conviction, that for us the Leader is, in all political and other matters concerning the national and social interests of the people, simply infallible. Wherein lies the secret of this enormous influence which he has on his followers? . . . It is something mystical, inexpressible, almost incomprehensible, which this unique man possesses, and he who cannot feel it instinctively will not be able to grasp it at all. For we love Adolf Hitler, because we believe deeply and unswervingly that God has sent him to us to save Germany.[3]

A similar attitude also existed in Italy where Mussolini was proclaimed as a genius, a creative force who united in his person the

3. Hermann Goering, *Germany Reborn* (London, 1934), pp. 79–80.

irrational elements of the will of history, a man in the Messianic sense who was also the exemplary Italian in whom the people found its representative.[4] A Turkish reading book for adults, referring to Mustafa Kemal, says:

> There is in creation much that is beautiful, much that is fine. But the most beautiful and the finest of all is a perfect human being. To feel this from the heart it is only necessary to be, even for a short time, in the presence of the great Gazi.[5]

Another writer says that although it is possible to concentrate on a number of reforms carried through by Marshal Pilsudski, the dictator of Poland, "we prefer to contemplate the man himself, his features, gestures and deeds, standing out against the background of his people and of the distracted and tormented continent of Europe. . . . His figure is the embodiment of greatness, grace and heroism combined with simplicity." [6]

Although the theory of historic materialism denies that an individual can have any influence on the progress of events, the same phenomenon has occurred in the Soviet Union. Although Beatrice and Sidney Webb did not consider Stalin a dictator, they found "the deliberate exploitation by the governing junta of the emotion of hero-worship, of the traditional reverence of the Russian people for a personal autocrat. . . . Scarcely a speech is made or a conference held, without a naïve—some would say a fulsome—reference to 'Comrade Stalin' as the great leader of the people." [7] At the time when the Webbs wrote, the deification of Lenin, which began soon after his death, had become a fixed feature of Soviet national life; and in the years that followed the prestige of Stalin rapidly increased. Now the embalmed bodies of both of these dead heroes are to be enshrined in an enlarged mausoleum so that people passing through may see them as they were in life.

It is well known that such sentiments are assiduously cultivated

4. Emilio Bodrero, "Mussolini and the Dictatorship in Italy," in Otto Forst de Battaglia (ed.), *Dictatorship on Its Trial* (translated by H. Patterson; London, 1930), esp. pp. 247–250; Herbert W. Schneider, *Making the Fascist State* (New York, 1928), pp. 125, 227.

5. Quoted in Spearman, *op. cit.*, pp. 83–84.

6. Forst de Battaglia, *op. cit.*, pp. 321–322.

7. *Soviet Communism: A New Civilisation?* (New York, Charles Scribner's Sons, 1936), p. 438. For a profound criticism of the Webbs on the ground that their ideas are anti-democratic, see Shirley R. Letwin, "Representation Without Democracy: The Webbs' Constitution," *The Review of Politics*, XVI (July, 1954), 352–375.

by a dictatorial regime. The press, radio, movies, and every conceivable means of communication are mobilized to hymn the praises of the all-wise ruler. It has been widely assumed that such statements are merely a propagandistic exaggeration, that hero-worship is a superstition which belongs to a past age, and that the adulation of a ruler by his subjects is nothing more than a form of flattery used by people to ingratiate themselves. However, extravagant statements of adoration are not confined to rulers in dictatorial countries. One is reminded of the American business man who said that President Franklin D. Roosevelt was "the greatest leader since Jesus Christ." [8] When one reads how thousands wept as they walked in the streets upon the death of Kemal Ataturk, how many of the common people were struck with a sincere grief by the passing of Stalin, or about the emotional feeling of many, if not most, Americans upon the death of President Franklin D. Roosevelt,[9] there can be no doubt about the existence of charisma. Power has a peculiar fascination to the human mind. The masses apparently dote on a leader who by the mystery of magnetism inspires respect, who makes himself into their national symbol, and who makes them feel great through their kinship with him. The belief in one man's power to perform miracles is undoubtedly promoted and encouraged by both the leader and his followers, but there is no question that millions do sincerely believe in it. The fact that the worship of the ruler is a recurring idea in history would also seem to indicate that the masses derive an emotional satisfaction in the experience of hero-worship. The question arises, therefore, as to what are the exigencies in contemporary life responsible for the return of personal leadership and the psychological conditions which have created it.

Every nation has its leaders, but in some countries personal leadership has played a more important role than in others. For example, English history is largely a history of the impersonal. It is concerned with the expansion of precedents and the development of institutions. England had no law-giver. There was instead a slow solidification of a body of law proceeding from the steady activity

8. John T. Flynn, "Other People's Money," *New Republic,* LXXXV (December 11, 1935), 129.
9. For a discussion, see Harold Orlansky, "Reactions to the Death of President Roosevelt," *The Journal of Social Psychology,* XXVI (1947), 235–266.

of the legal profession. Both German and Italian history show a more personal character. Although the making of the common law and the evolution of Parliament play a large role in English medieval history, the medieval history of Germany is concerned mainly with the achievements and failures of her kings and emperors. Italian history has also shown a more personal character. Both Italy and Germany have suffered from a long past of disunion, and personal figures have become the necessary symbols of national unity. Great and arresting personalities, such as Mazzini, Garibaldi, and Cavour, have deeply affected Italian life. Prussia was made by its electors and kings; and when in the latter half of the nineteenth century Prussia passed into Germany, it did so through the spirit and personality of Bismarck.

If the history of a country is largely understood as the history of great men, the idea of a "sleeping hero" who will come forth and save the situation has more appeal and is more likely to find acceptance. Even after making proper allowance for the fact that a part of the difference can be accounted for by the way in which the history of these countries has been written, there is no question that both German and Italian history have always shown a more personal character. The principle of personal leadership, therefore, was not a new and sudden eruption. The doctrine of the higher personality of the people, expressed and realized in the person of its leader, was a part of their thought because it found inspiration in their past. However, this old and historic character assumed a new form by entering into an alliance with the democratic factor of party and by creating a personal party following to serve the leader as the immediate source of acknowledgment and recognition.

It is obvious that many men must participate in the building and maintaining of a government and that a constitutional system can never be the work of one great leader. In Western Europe it took a long time for men to build an impersonal state acting through impersonal institutions and by impersonal rules of law. A democratic government which protects the claims and guarantees the rights of each individual is the last stage in this long period of development. However, even in democratic countries the masses have found it easier to fix their allegiance to a single personality than to a group of legislators whom it is hard to make responsible. Almost everywhere the executive has increased in power and prestige as compared with the legislature; and although this development is to some extent the inevitable result of social and economic changes which have produced a tremendous growth in the functions and activities of government, it has also been furthered by an extension of the suffrage. In both Britain and the United States the exploitation of personality has gone on increasingly as the franchise was widened to include a larger number of citizens. Ever since the days of Gladstone and Disraeli British electors have tended to vote for individual candidates, not on their merits, but in terms of whom they will support to be the prime minister. This development has also been furthered by the increased use of the press and radio. Today everything that a British prime minister or an American president says or does is news. Every party must have a great leader, and in the hands of the publicity experts he becomes almost divinely inspired.

> Poor Mr. Baldwin, an honest and kindly man, but not by any means, a superman, has had to submit to a painful process of inflation, and to see his gently quizzical head reproduced in gigantic posters on every hoarding in the land, over the inspiring motto 'Safety First'; he has had to permit his pipe and his pigs to be used as symbols. Mr. Ramsay MacDonald has had to subdue his aversion from publicity: he has had to let the Press know what he reads when he travels by aeroplane; when he goes upon his travels across the Atlantic he has to endure the society of a troop of journalists, who, whenever he takes a walk on deck, send the glad news home by wireless; he has to pose to the 'movies' and the 'talkies' —with whatever reluctance—as the weary Titan, bearing the cares of empire with a sad, brave smile.[10]

In the same manner the eyes of the entire nation are fixed upon the President of the United States. The masses expect him to manage Congress and to secure favorable action on a well-rounded legislative program. Rightly or wrongly they tend to give him all the credit for successes but they also blame him for all the failures or shortcomings during his administration whether they can be attributed to his own personal actions or not.

Any one who has taught history can appreciate the difficulty involved in raising the level of historical analysis from a study of great personalities to a study of movements. There is something

10. Ramsay Muir, *How Britain Is Governed* (Fourth edition; Boston and New York, 1940), pp. 120–121.

captivating about the heroic figure, and there is always a temptation even on the part of the most sophisticated scholar to personalize. In the primary grades the student is first introduced to the great personalities in history, and it is only as he grows older and more advanced that he is able to graduate to a study of issues and institutions apart from personality.

The development of science has brought with it an increasing emphasis on specialization, and this process also contributes to charisma. For example, an engineer may be a genius in his field; but he has his own prejudices and superstitions and may not know much about politics. As a result, he may be impressed by the demagogue and lend the prestige of his position in the community in support of such a movement. Moreover, the increasing utilization of experts in the various specialized fields creates a temptation to consult an "expert" in the field of politics. Democracy presupposes that the elements of public opinion grow out of knowledge and that they are the product of reason, and modern democratic thinkers have tended to assume that the more educated a democracy is the better will its government be. However, there was no better educated nation than Germany. An increase in education and specialization do not necessarily produce an increased rationalization. As Lord Bryce pointed out long before the rise of Hitler,

> Attainments in learning and science do little to make men wise in politics. Some eminent scientific men have been in this respect no wiser than their undergraduate pupils. There have been countries in which the chiefs of public services and the professors in Universities were prominent in the advocacy of policies which proved disastrous.[11]

Of course, knowledge is always better than ignorance, but the ability to read is only a gateway to knowledge and reading is not a substitute for thinking. Democracy presupposes a nation with

11. *Modern Democracies*, I, 78. "Unguarded either by belief in an ancient creed, or by a rational study of the problems of social life, the expert is ready to fall a victim to any new heresy. He will seize on any gospel that has the appearance of providing a safe orthodoxy on which to base the crumbling state, so long as it is presented by demagogues sufficiently clever or by tyrants sufficiently powerful. . . . In these conditions it is not difficult to understand why the general acceptance of the principle of universal education, and the great advance of specialist studies, should have been accompanied by the rise of dictatorship and the development of the totalitarian state. . . . It is the educated, not the uneducated masses, who form the real problem in the modern state." Alfred Cobban, *Dictatorship, Its History and Theory* (New York, 1939), pp. 240–241.

sound judgment, with the power to get at the facts and argue con-
secutively from them, with the capacity to reflect and judge, and
with a devotion to the common interest. In other words, knowledge
is only one among the many things which go into the making of a
good citizen, and increased educational opportunity has not always
produced an increase in political education. In so far as the growth
of large cities have reduced the opportunity for personal participation by the citizen in local self-government, an important training
ground of democracy has been lost; and in so far as modern education has failed to produce a well-rounded individual capable of
critically analyzing political issues and devoted to participating in
community life and taking an active interest in civic affairs, it has
failed to produce the type of man upon which democracy depends.

FREUDIAN CONCEPTIONS

Sigmund Freud, the founder of psychoanalysis, developed a
theory of human nature and behavior which, when given an application to social problems, has challenged the older forms of social
psychology and produced new insights for explaining the emergence
of dictatorship.[12] Space does not permit an extensive discussion of
Freud's ideas and the social and political implications involved.
However, his most important contribution lies in the emphasis he
placed upon unconscious motivation and the role of irrational
factors in human conduct. His discoveries have caused us to revise
our conception of human nature and to see more clearly wherein
the democratic theorists of the eighteenth and nineteenth centuries
held a much too simple and optimistic view of man and placed too
great an emphasis upon his rational nature.

Freud's psychology of society starts from the experience of the
individual. There is developed inside the human psyche a father-
hatred because it is the father who intervenes and prevents the child
from possessing mother completely. In some respects the father is a
terrible figure because it is he who brings the element of fear into
a child's life through punishment and who teaches him a consciousness of guilt. At the same time, the child has a feeling of respect

12. Freud's most important books which make direct contributions to the
social sciences are: *Group Psychology and the Analysis of the Ego* (London,
1922); *The Future of an Illusion* (London, 1928); *Civilization and Its Discontents*
(London, 1930); and *The Problem of Anxiety* (New York, 1936).

and admiration for the father, and this hate-love attitude is called ambivalence. The father is the most powerful member of the family; he is generally a kindly and benevolent person; the child is dependent on the father for the necessities of life and indeed thinks of him at first as an all-powerful person.

In the normal family an equilibrium is reached, but in every individual the experience of his early years is entangled with his whole personality. After he becomes an adult, he often wishes that he could return to his childhood when all of his wants were satisfied without effort on his part. After leaving the all-embracing comforts of the home, he is constantly seeking the loving mother and the father whom he respects and admires. Thus the king is an unconscious symbol of the father and the queen of the mother. A successful statesman has frequently been called "the father of his country." It is possible to substitute a symbol or an idea for an individual, but in times of stress and strain a people may not remain content with a "symbolic" leader and demand the destruction of the institutions standing between them and emotional reality. It may be that they will demand a "savior" or a "leader" who will stand in the same emotional relationship to them as that in which a father used to stand. Thus freedom is not really what people want, and dictatorship is merely the effort of a strained people to bring about order. It is the result of an emotional need which people feel, especially at a time when political conditions appear to be outside of human control, for a dominating personality.

If such a theory explains the existence of dictators, it does not explain why some periods are democratic and others are autocratic or why men have ever escaped from the domination of some father figure. It would appear that the answer lies in changing political conditions. In a period of stability the average person is not much interested in politics and statesmen do not arouse deep-felt emotions in the majority of those they govern. The absence of feeling and the presence of an objective disinterestedness gives reason a greater opportunity. However, in periods of violent conflict when people see the world which they have known melting away political events become a matter of immense importance. If men are cold, hungry, and impoverished and if there is also a vast incomprehensible menace, such as an economic crisis or war, they are seized by a paralyzing fear because the situation seems to leave no room for action.

The very nature of the crisis makes an individual feel helpless and like a little child. He is inhibited from taking any action on his own because he does not know what is happening; and even if sources of information are available to the ordinary person, he is incapable of understanding.

> How could the Turkish peasant understand the complications of the world situation in 1922, the Italian the economic crisis, the Russian the famine and civil war which swept over him, the German worker the complex results of war and economic crisis? He is reduced to the position of a child in an incomprehensible world; his reaction resembles that of the ordinary adult in the face of illness.[13]

Freud thought that the special pattern of family relationships into which an individual had to fit himself in the earliest years of his life was responsible for a variety of personality types. A new-born child at first has little consciousness of itself but possesses inherited instincts, urges, and physical desires. The blind aggressive and unconscious drive to satisfy these wants Freud called the id. As the world is impressed upon the id, it becomes conscious of itself and a basic modification begins. The ego, or self, is thought of as being built upon the id. It is partly conscious and partly unconscious and receives ideas from the id as well as impressions from the external world. As the child develops still further, he comes into contact with parental attitudes and tends to make them his own. For example, the child wants something but the parents won't let him have what he wants; rage ensues; and the parents are disappointed. The child is made to feel that if he wants love he must act in a certain way and that he may have to do some things he doesn't want to do. Experiences of this kind build attitude. However, in so far as this attitude condemns instinctual urges it arouses and maintains a sense of guilt. Freud called the conscience, or guilt-sense, the super-ego. He thought of it as an outgrowth and modification of the ego but as independent and inaccessible to the conscious ego. It is in contact with and serves as a restraining influence on the aggressive id. Thus the unconscious id under the impact of the external world becomes differentiated into a partly conscious and partly unconscious ego and an unconscious super-ego. Id, ego, and super-ego form three dynamic systems whose inner conflicts, together with

13. Spearman, *Modern Dictatorship,* p. 104.

the manner in which they are adjusted to one another and to the external world, make up the subsequent life history of the individual.

In the normal personality an equilibrium is reached which involves a maximum of pleasure and a minimum of pain, but such an equilibrium is always precarious. Amid changing demands of the outer world, the ego must maintain an inner condition which prevents both undue pressure from the id and undue repression from the super-ego. This can be done even in the most normal personality only through the establishment of a variety of behavior patterns which need only to become a little exaggerated and dominant to cause abnormality. These behavior patterns are the ego's defense mechanisms against upset. They involve the establishment of substitute channels for the discharge of sexual energy or for the transformation of the energy itself. Difficulties of adjustment, for example, may lead to the return to an earlier or lower level of development, as in the case of "fixation," or to the efforts of repressed ideas arising from the levels of the unconscious id to reach consciousness in other ways than those closed by the super-ego. Thus "projection" consists in externalizing repressed wishes and ideas whose conscious acceptance by the individual would be painful.

One of the most remarkable of Freud's clinical discoveries was how phobias in the mind can be projected on external objects. An individual may have a deep inner conflict; but instead of a clash inside, it can be fixed on an object outside. This attitude has nothing to do with honesty. The internal difficulty is so grave that an object outside appears to be the menace. As a matter of fact, it was the discovery of "transference" which caused Freud to undertake psychoanalysis.

The more strict the family upbringing the more there is a suppressed hate drive and the more there is a desire to unload hatred on other people. For example, there is the tough sergeant in the army because of the strict training in the army. Whenever male dominance is marked, the more likely there is to be a severe hate drive. In this connection a number of observers have noted that German society is characterized by the glorification of maleness, strict family life, severe thrashings in the schools, and a suicide rate the highest in Europe. In every individual there is the aggressive impulse to get things and the super-ego, or the guilt sense. The tension between the perfection side and the id side may be so great that a people will demand a leader to lead them. The leader can take the burden of guilt on his shoulders; and if he preaches war, id can have its outlet too. Many have told how happy they were in identifying themselves with Hitler.[14]

APPLICATION OF FREUDIAN DOCTRINES

A more comprehensive application of Freud's ideas to political phenomena in general and to the emergence of dictatorship in particular has been attempted by a number of writers. For example, some have discovered neurotic tendencies in a whole society;[15] others have attributed psychoses to a particular class;[16] and still others have attempted to psychoanalyze the leaders.[17] Although the "intellectual techniques" suggested by economic determinism and psychoanalysis are fundamentally in opposition to one another, certain other writers have attempted to bridge the gap and combine them both.[18] However, the failure of these authors to agree upon the facts and the confusion resulting from their contradictory findings have given rise to the charge that the psychiatrist can "prove anything" when he deals with groups rather than individuals. Most writers, realizing that society molds and shapes a man's character, have a combined socio-psychological approach.[19] However, such a method when taken alone does not increase our knowledge of totalitarian movements. For example, the studies made at the University of California on the authoritarian personality are important and the work itself is valuable in so far as it increases our knowledge of man and his relationship to society.[20] However, if it is argued that

14. Hadley Cantril, *The Psychology of Social Movements* (New York, 1941), pp. 233–270; Abel, *op. cit.;* Schuman, *op. cit.,* esp. pp. 122–124.
15. Richard M. Brickner, *Is Germany Incurable?* (New York, 1943). The central contention is that the paranoid elements in the population have increasingly dominated the non-paranoid elements until a condition has been reached in which the majority of Germans are, from the point of view of the psychiatrist, homicidally insane.
16. Frederick L. Schuman, *The Nazi Dictatorship* (New York, 1939); Harold D. Lasswell, "The Psychology of Hitlerism," *The Political Quarterly,* IV (1933), 374.
17. G. M. Gilbert, *The Psychology of Dictatorship* (New York, 1950).
18. R. Osborn, *The Psychology of Reaction* (London, 1938).
19. See, for example, Cantril, *op. cit.;* Erich Fromm, *Escape from Freedom* (New York, 1942).
20. T. W. Adorno, Else Frenkel-Brunswick, Nevitt Sanford, and D. Levinson, *The Authoritarian Personality* (New York, 1950).

an authoritarian personality is likely to support a totalitarian movement, this in itself does not explain why and how the Nazis and the Fascists, for example, became mass parties; for it was not their regular following but the added support which they received that turned these parties into mass movements. Moreover, there is some reason to doubt whether an authoritarian personality will actually join a totalitarian movement. Although the necessary comparative evidence is lacking to answer this question properly, it may be that an authoritarian personality, who is generally uncooperative and anti-social, will be unable to compromise his own position so as to make it possible for him to join a mass movement. In addition, the mere existence of such personalities in a given society does not necessarily prove anything, for the bigotry and intolerance of such men may cancel each other out.

Psychiatric theories are based on empirical evidence derived from therapy, and hence they tend to have a "pathological" bias. The psychiatrist knows that neurotic symptoms are an individual's way of expressing and disguising his failure to solve successfully the problems posed for him by his environment. He also knows that the cumulative experiences of every patient account for the formation of specific symptoms, but he does not know that the same experiences will lead to similar symptoms in all cases. At every stage in his development a child is confronted with the task of "coming to terms" with his environment and resolving a multitude of problems. Some children will succeed in making the proper adjustment; others will fail. The psychiatrist, who is interested in the origin of neurotic symptoms, concentrates on those who failed. He knows that there is a clear syndrome of character traits which *may* arise from this or that source, but he cannot confidently predict that the difficulties which have created neurotic symptoms in the one case will do the same in most cases. The therapist comes into contact with people who are distinguished from the general population in that they have decided to seek his help, and hence he has little opportunity to test his findings with a "control group." Psychiatric theories derived from biographical data taken from individual patients do not permit valid sociological generalizations because an effort to extend them to a whole group or a whole society compels an unwarranted "systematic bias in favor of determinism and against a recognition of the important role which choices and accidents play in the development of the human personality." [21] A psychological interpretation of cultural patterns, therefore, has only a limited utility because it seeks to integrate basically inconsistent elements.

The careful study of Nazi Germany made by Paul Kecskemeti and Nathan Leites offers a good illustration of the difficulties involved.[22] The authors pointed out that Nazi propaganda emphasized will power, endurance, hardness, discipline, devotion, hard work, and sacrifice, and that these traits correspond to the "compulsive character" type of psychoanalytic literature. The significance of their study for our purposes lies in how this correspondence is to be interpreted. Kecskemeti and Leites differ from most other writers in the field in that they carefully list in the introductory section of their article a number of reservations. For example, one cannot say (1) that psychological factors, including infantile experiences, are the sole or even the main cause for the widespread development of compulsive traits among Germans; (2) that the hypotheses advanced have been fully confirmed because this can be done "only in the psychoanalytic interview situation"; (3) that the conclusions reached are valid for the periods before or after the Nazi regime; (4) that "major transformations of the political structure of Germany are incompatible with present character structures"; (5) that there were not other (than the compulsive) types of character structure among both adherents and opponents of the Nazi regime.[23] Taking into consideration these and other reservations, the position of the authors appears to be that Nazi propaganda had a special appeal to those whose personalities predisposed them to accept its slogans. Those segments of the German people most likely to exhibit the syndrome of the compulsive personality were:

> It may be safely said that it was more widely diffused among *lower middle class* persons than among persons higher up or lower down in the class system; among *males* than among females; among those who had been adolescents *before or around* 1933 than among those who were so afterwards; in *Northern Germany* than in Southern Germany; among

21. Reinhard Bendix, "Compliant Behavior and Individual Personality," *The American Journal of Sociology*, LVIII (1952), 294. This is a learned and thought-provoking study. Many of my conclusions are based on this article.
22. "Some Psychological Hypotheses on Nazi Germany," *Journal of Social Psychology*, XXVI (1947), 141–183; XXVII (February, 1948), 91–117; (May, 1948), 241–270; (August, 1948), 141–164.
23. *Ibid.*, XXVI, 141–144.

Protestants than among Catholics; among *city people* than among country people; among *political followers* than among political leaders.[24]

In spite of these and other reservations the authors assume that people respond to cultural symbols because of their character structure. People act as they do because their personality traits predispose them to do so. Since Nazi propaganda displayed characteristics analogous to the compulsive personality, it is assumed that those who were attracted by it also possessed those traits. Of course, this could not be proved without examining the life histories of the individuals concerned to determine whether they did in fact develop a compulsion neurosis. Such a view also presumes that specific neurotic symptoms are widespread and that they are both the cause and consequence of certain cultural symbols. In a sense this constitutes a kind of circular reasoning because "certain symbols of a culture (e.g., Nazi propaganda) are the basis on which the character structure of particular groups in German society is inferred, and this inference is then used to show why the symbols had such wide appeal." [25]

The fact that an individual responds to these symbols does not necessarily reveal their meaning for him nor his reason in doing so. It is well known that there were significant differences among the responses of a Prussian Junker, a Bavarian separatist, a Nazi functionary, and a German Communist; yet all may have had compulsive personalities. People respond favorably to cultural symbols because they are expected to do so. They accept propaganda slogans sometimes because of fear, sometimes because of ignorance, at other times through apathy, and for many other reasons *in spite of,* as well as *because of,* their psychological disposition. In other words, if cultural symbols are analyzed in terms of psychological analogies, there is a tendency to attribute to psychological disposition what may be the result of economic pressure, political power, or historical tradition.

Those who seek to "explain" the rise of dictatorship in terms of national character have pointed out that National Socialism is related to other authoritarian aspects of German society. Since modern psychiatry emphasizes the importance of an individual's early

24. *Ibid.,* p. 143.
25. Bendix, *op. cit.,* p. 297.

experience in the development of personality, the authoritarian pattern of German family life has come in for a great deal of criticism. For example, it is argued that children raised in such an environment are likely to be more "submissive" and that the authoritarian family was, therefore, a major reason for the rise of fascism.

This theory fails to take cognizance of the fact that the Nazis themselves took a dim view of the political reliability of the German family and adopted a number of policies which were designed to lessen its authority and to destroy its influence. For example, they organized children into youth movements, encouraged them to spy on their parents, and subjected them to authority figures outside of the family which could be controlled politically. Leaders of totalitarian movements almost universally consider the family a seedbed of resistance because even the authoritarian family is a conservative force opposed to major social and political change. In the Soviet Union as well as in other communist regimes a reluctant adult population is held in line by making their children enthusiastic supporters of the government.

It is undoubtedly true that Germans are more authoritarian than Americans, but this fact cannot be explained by describing in the language of psychiatry the ideas and actions a group of people have in common and thus making it appear as though they are the actions of an individual person. For example, American life is strongly anti-authoritarian, yet it emphasizes conventionality, a trait which is compatible with the compulsive personality. On the other hand, German life combines a spirit of strong individualism with being authoritarian. There is no data to support the view that the shared conventional patterns of behavior in a culture are indicative of the character structure of a people.[26] In every society large numbers of people have certain problems and certain conventional behavior patterns in common, but it cannot be proved that they make a common response to these problems or conventions. Men accommodate themselves to their environment and to social change as best they can, but the response of each individual is likely to depend upon his own character structure as this is related to childhood experience. In every society men engage in the type of behavior others expect of them, but it does not follow that they "desire to act as they have

26. This appears to be the position taken by Erich Fromm. See *Escape from Freedom*, pp. 277, 283–285.

to act" or that beneath the conventions imposed by institutions and traditions that their response is the same. It would be more reasonable to assume that there are a wide range of responses which roughly correspond to the range of personality types.

If this analysis is correct, generalizations about personality are culture-limited. Standards of mental health pertaining to people in one society cannot be applied to those in another. The temptation to attribute to people in another culture a psychological uniformity lacking in our own must somehow be resisted as well as the danger of finding in the character structure what may be a part of the social environment.

The government of a country can be profitably studied only in terms of the whole complex of traditions, institutions, ideologies, and experiences of the people concerned. Events involving war or peace, economic depression or prosperity, political stability or instability have significant psychological repercussions; but their effect on a group of persons cannot be explained by resorting to analogies drawn from the terminology of psychiatry. If the forces making for social and cultural changes are to be understood, it is necessary to "discover in each society the diversity of responses which is hidden beneath the uniformity of conventional behavior that is 'apparent' to the outside observer." [27]

THE MASS STATE

Some observers, noting that an individual is less rational in a crowd than when acting alone, see modern dictatorship as a political system which rests on amorphous masses. It is argued that conditions in our age tend to fuse people into a mass and that this mass is inimical to democracy. José Ortega y Gasset was one of the first to present this point of view,[28] but he tended to identify the increasing numbers of society with the mass and to cast suspicion on every association of the many by calling it a crowd or mass. In doing so, he failed to distinguish between a mob and those groups which raise, rather than lower, the mental level of their members. His book is largely a protest against the imposition of mass judgments and standards not merely in the political world but in the cultural

27. Bendix, *op. cit.*, p. 301.
28. *The Revolt of the Masses* (New York, 1932). See also the earlier work of Gustave Le Bon, *The Crowd: A Study of the Popular Mind* (London, 1897).

world as well. Thus he joins those critics of modern democracy who find in mass mediocrity, incompetence, and stupidity the greatest menace to Western civilization.

A somewhat different point of view, although similar in its basic conception, has been presented by Emil Lederer.[29] Unlike Ortega y Gasset he differentiates between the mass or crowd which is socially amorphous and held together by emotion and other social groups which are homogeneous and held together by a common bond of interest. The mass or crowd has a sort of dynamism of its own, is composed of people who inwardly act together, but can become articulate only through a tyrannical leader because it can find unity only in terms of the most primitive emotions. The leader of this mass is an emotional man who knows how to take advantage of the situation and who can voice the feelings of the masses or at least make them feel that his thoughts are theirs. Although crowds have often played a part in history, their role has heretofore been a transitory one. However, in Communist Russia, Fascist Italy, and Nazi Germany men have experienced the first emergence of the new mass state. It is a political system which institutionalizes the masses, "making them a political and social steamroller, crushing social groups of every kind. . . . there has never been a state which destroyed the social structure to such an extent, and there has never been a time which offered the technical opportunities of today to transform the whole people into masses and to keep them in this state." [30] The extent to which the traditional classes had served as a means of integrating society through their disciplines, ideas, and interests was not appreciated until after fascism had destroyed them. Moreover, the extent to which freedom and justice were guaranteed by the tension and balance between competing groups was not understood until totalitarianism transformed the population into masses.

It follows that functional groups and classes of all kinds must be maintained. The classless society of Marx's dreams is the worst evil that could come to Western civilization because it must "transform the population into masses and create a mass-state just as

29. *State of the Masses: The Threat of the Classless Society* (New York, 1940).
30. *Ibid.*, pp. 45–46.

fascist dictatorships do." [31] In Hitler's Germany and Mussolini's Italy the triumph of the mass over differentiation of the mass produced a new tyranny and the possibility of a new exploitation which had heretofore been thought to be impossible. Fascism is built on the masses and commanded by leaders who keep them in an emotional stage. It destroys society and aims at melting it into a crowd. In order to do this, the independent existence of every group in society, free speech, and free thinking must be destroyed. There is thus no group or institution in society which might furnish opposition, and the people are manipulated through the clever use of propaganda. If the masses continue to be the only force in society, everything worthwhile will be destroyed. The conception of a classless society came before we understood fully the implications of the new mass state.

Dr. Lederer's analysis emphasizes the unique nature of modern dictatorships and focuses attention upon the importance of the free interplay of spontaneous and responsible group associations as a necessary precondition for social order. Both communist and fascist states seek to transform these groups into agents of the state and atomize the subject population. In a sense Lederer substitutes the balancing powers of clashing classes for the classical liberal belief in a preordained social harmony of rational human beings as the guarantor of freedom; and in doing so he adopts the view that individuals, apart from the group to which they belong, are capable only of irrational attitudes and emotional epidemics. Although democratic political thinkers have tended to overestimate man's power of rational thought, it may be that Lederer's appraisal exaggerates emotion and the irrational aspects of human conduct. In any case, he merely shows how a totalitarian movement can corrupt a whole nation after it achieves power; but he does not explain what forces are responsible for the disintegration of society in the first place. If fascism and communism are the product of social crisis, then the successful operation of democracy obviously requires much more than a restoration of pre-dictatorial stratified society. Moreover, there is a distinction between a stratification which produces cooperating social groups and a class society composed of bitter warring factions. Every form of social stratification is not an expres-

31. *Ibid.*, p. 151.

sion of class society and class war. If democracy is to be preserved, we need to know more about how to achieve cooperation between the classes and how to avoid social bitterness and class war.

VALIDITY OF THESE INSIGHTS

In most of the discussion in this chapter the level of abstraction is high, and hence it is difficult to test the validity of these theories in terms of empirical fact. However, if they are treated properly they do offer new insights for a better understanding of contemporary conditions. There are many conflicting schools of thought among contemporary psychologists; and a leading authority, after examining seven contemporary schools, tells us that there is "no one interpretation of the facts of psychology to which all psychologists, or even a majority, agree." [32] However, the same author says that "there is a notable agreement among psychologists that the rational and cognitive sides of human nature have been enormously over-emphasized in the past." [33]

Although the psychoanalytical approach is frequently revealing when applied to individuals and often provides valuable data towards a better understanding of political leaders, there is considerable reason to doubt whether it can be intelligently used to explain a whole cultural pattern. Moreover, authors attempting to use this method do not apply it in the same way and do not agree upon the facts. For example, Frederick L. Schuman thinks that Hitler disliked his mother as well as his father because she "spoke with a Czechish accent." [34] On the other hand, Professor G. M. Gilbert thinks that he loved his mother and hated his father and speaks of "an Oedipus complex." [35] The facts themselves could perhaps be clarified by further research; but the important point suggested by this contradiction is that it probably occurred in the first place because of a desire to use the psychoanalytical method. Although isolated facts are meaningless and although it is necessary to show a relationship between them in order to increase understanding,

32. Edna Heidbreder, *Seven Psychologies* (New York, 1933), p. 413.
33. *Ibid.*, p. 418.
34. *The Nazi Dictatorship*, pp. 6–7. On page 8 Professor Schuman says that Hitler "hated Slavs—and yet he probably had no realization that he was here giving expression to his contempt for his mother and for something deep in himself."
35. *The Psychology of Dictatorship*, pp. 18–25.

still an enthusiastic desire to apply a "new method" may lead to the fabrication of facts or a misrepresentation of events in order to illustrate the validity of this "approach" to the subject. In the last analysis, there is no substitute for the careful accumulation of data, and there is no reason to strain for the adoption of a new "conceptual framework" to explain the rise of dictatorship. In so far as psychology has made a contribution it has reminded us of facts which were already known and in so far as it has provided insights capable of being tested by empirical data it merely reiterates principles already noted by leading political philosophers.

If men in times of crisis seek the domination of a father figure, it ought to be added that in periods of prosperity and stability they are likely to revolt against an autocratic ruler and to demand the right to participate in government. When men feel helpless and alone, they are likely to be submissive; but when these factors are lacking, they are likely to be resentful of authority and to favor a relaxation of restrictions. Modern psychiatry and the insights which it provides into the irrational factors and the persistently aggressive features of basic human nature furnish only a partial approach for the study of political behavior. History records many instances when the play of rational purposes, the willingness to sacrifice for an ideal cause, and a spirit of benevolence and cooperation have played a dominant role. After all, as Diana Spearman has said, "If men in reality behave, not according to any rational standards, but according to whether they loved or hated their parents, then they are incapable of being improved by any discussion whatever." [36] The same, of course, is true if the human mind simply consists of automatic reactions to outside stimuli.

It would be ridiculous to argue that the accumulated psychological data based upon painstaking research is of no value. However, it is the application of these data largely by political scientists and the conclusions drawn, which are not demonstrated by facts, that is at fault. Most psychologists have been extremely hesitant about drawing political conclusions from their researches, and those who know most about the subject have given little support to the sweeping generalizations made by others. The fact of the matter is that we do not yet know much about the springs of human behavior,

36. *Modern Dictatorship,* p. 168.

of the influence of fear on action, and of the difference between the behavior of individuals in isolation and in groups. Until further progress has been made in the field of psychology we must guard against hasty generalizations.

It is often said that human nature is always and everywhere the same; yet the truth is that in many essential matters it differs. Psychiatry finds that there is usually a reason in an individual's experience which helps explain his subsequent conduct. In the same way, there are reasons why nations think and behave the way they do. What we need to know is more about the factors that have influenced their institutional development and the reasons why they hold the values that they do. Freud and his school are to be congratulated for having emphasized the complexity and irrationality of human motives. However, an attempt to show that the conduct of particular nations is similar to that of an individual suffering from a neurosis does not increase our understanding and does not tell us what we need to know if we are to better understand the nature of and the reasons for totalitarian movements.

THE NATURE OF DEMOCRACY

I N THE preceding chapters emphasis has been placed upon the factors inherent in modern society that have contributed to or are at least partially responsible for the rise of dictatorship. Absolutism does not represent a complete break with the past as has sometimes been supposed. There is a "democratic tradition" in the Western world but it is blended with dictatorial elements; and there is an "authoritarian tradition" as well. Moreover, there is considerable confusion and lack of precision in our thinking concerning the nature of democracy and the underlying assumptions upon which it is based. Every modern government is faced with tremendous problems which are not easily resolved, but their solution within the framework of democracy requires not only an ability to adapt institutions fashioned for a different type of world but also a better understanding of democracy itself.

DEMOCRACY AND EQUALITY

Both friends and enemies have contended that democracy means equality and that it is inconsistent with the existence of social classes. Thus Plato criticized democracy in the *Republic* because it "gives a sort of equality to equals and unequals alike." [1] A number of modern writers have turned this accusation into a vindication of democracy and argue that the decline of democracy is due to its failure to provide a greater social equality. For example,

1. Book IX, 558.

Harold J. Laski, believing that a true democracy is synonymous with egalitarian socialism, wrote:

> The discipline of capitalist democracy is in decay because the principle of capitalism cannot be squared with the principle of democracy. The one consistently seeks to maintain inequalities which the other, not less consistently, seeks to abolish.[2]

Those who hold that democracy implies the abolition of social classes do not base this opinion upon an observation of facts but base it instead upon either a fear of popular rule or else upon emotional belief in a socialist state. History records no instance in which any government has been able to secure an absolute social equality. Social classes have existed in every democratic society from ancient times to the present, and democratic political institutions have functioned in societies which differed considerably in their social structures. For example, American society was predominantly agrarian in the early years of the republic, but it has become overwhelmingly urban today. The conservative statesmen in the nineteenth century, who like Disraeli favored extending the suffrage because they thought the lower classes would support conservative politics, did not believe that they were thereby promoting social equality. History also records a number of instances of restricted democracy in which portions of the population were excluded from the exercise of political rights. Even slavery has existed along side of democratic institutions in both ancient and modern times. There is no necessary connection between democracy and any specific principle of social evaluation. It is possible for people to accept and believe in social distinctions and economic inequalities and still remain attached to democratic institutions.

There is a sense in which equality is a part of the democratic tradition. The American Declaration of Independence maintains that "all men are created equal," and the slogan of the French Revolution was "liberty, equality, and fraternity." It is, of course, a matter of common observation that men are not born equal, that they vary in physical size and intelligence, and that they differ in position, influence, power, or authority. No government has ever succeeded in making men equal in these respects. On the other hand, democracy makes men equal as citizens, gives them equality

2. *Democracy in Crisis*, p. 215.

as voting units, guarantees to them equality before the law, and gives them freedom to speak their minds and to organize in the pursuit of their interests. Democracy was born as a protest against special privilege and may do much to give each individual the opportunity to develop without prejudice or other impediment his knowledge, talent, or creative genius; but it cannot guarantee an equality of attainment, status, wealth, or social position. Even if men were born equal, it is certain that they are not content to stay that way. As Professor R. M. MacIver has said,

> To keep men equal in wealth, in spite of their unequal abilities and varying aptitudes, would require a degree of all-round regimentation vastly surpassing anything that dynast or tyrant or dictator has hitherto accomplished. Even the ideal of total equality is a superficial mechanical one, contrary to the nature of things, having no relationship to intrinsic spiritual values, utterly unlike the ideal of democracy. It is indeed dangerous to confuse or identify the two.[3]

It is an interesting fact that dictatorships have been more successful than democracies in promoting social equality. This is because an autocratic government tends to level down social distinctions and to substitute for them personal distinctions based upon equal dependence and subjection. Hans Speier says that "such a policy is part of the political logic of autocracies" because gradations in social status indicate gradations of actual or potential power and hence an incomplete subjection to the dictatorship. Since autocracy never promotes exemptions from its domination, the effect of its policies may be to destroy former class distinctions and promote a kind of social equality. Thus "the more closely social equality is approached, the less important become democratic institutions; the more differentiated and stratified society, the greater the mischief of dictatorial government and, conversely, the more imperative is democracy for a just and judicious form of political life."[4]

In the Soviet Union social classes have not been abolished and a "classless society" has not been achieved. The socialization of industry and the collectivization of agriculture destroyed traditional class

3. *The Ramparts We Guard* (New York, 1950), pp. 14–15.
4. Hans Speier, "Social Stratification," in Max Ascoli and Fritz Lehmann (eds.), *Political and Economic Democracy* (New York, 1937), p. 259. See also Heald, *op. cit.*, pp. 66–70.

distinctions, but they did not and could not abolish social class. Instead there is a new class system in which distinction is based, not so much on birth and wealth, as upon the nearness and remoteness from political power. An overwhelming proportion of the leaders in public life are drawn from the party membership, and with the passage of time the percentage of industrial executives and administrators drawn from party lists has shown a tendency to increase. Soviet statistics announced in 1936 show that the percentage of factory directors who were party members had risen from 29 in 1923 to one hundred in 1931 and stood at 97.5 in the year of the report.[5] In a socialized economy the management of factories ranks next in importance to the direct control of public affairs, and with greater power goes greater prestige, greater opportunity, and greater privilege. Since the Communist party exercises a general supervision over every aspect of the social and economic life of the community, it is obvious that those who are outside the party must be content with a lower status. As Professor R. M. MacIver says:

> In a word, there is a new class system. Those who deny this conclusion either refuse, in the face of evidence, to admit that a class system can exist except on an economic basis or else they plainly believe that the inveterate expressions of human nature no longer manifest themselves under a collectivistic regime.[6]

The successful operation of democracy requires a harmonious and beneficial balance between the ideals of liberty and equality. As Professor William E. Rappard says,

> There is no doubt that the greater the measure of individual liberty maintained by the state in the modern world, the higher the degree of social

5. Barrington Moore, Jr., "The Communist Party of the Soviet Union: 1928–1944," *American Sociological Review*, IX (1944), 267–278. The fact that party membership is heavily weighted on the side of managerial personnel and that the party apparatus inside a plant is frequently little more than a part of the industrial administration has been the subject of discussion at a number of party congresses and conferences. At the Nineteenth Party Congress, held shortly before Premier Stalin's death, G. M. Malenkov charged that some party executives selected cadres "not by their political and professional qualifications, but by considerations of kinship, friendship, and cronyism" and that this situation had "given rise in some organizations to the formation of a closed circle of people who shield one another and who place the interests of their group above those of the Party and state." See Merle Fainsod, *How Russia Is Ruled* (Cambridge, Mass., 1953), pp. 201–239; Gregory Bienstock, Solomon M. Schwarz, and Aaron Yugow, *Management in Russian Industry and Agriculture* (New York, 1944), pp. 17–31, 104–124.

6. *The Web of Government*, p. 125.

inequality which will result therefrom. And, conversely, the greater the measure of equality imposed on a modern society by political authority, the narrower the margin of liberty left to the individual. In this conflict . . . modern democracy is tending more and more to sacrifice liberty to equality. . . . Its normal development and indeed its future depend on its ability to maintain a wholesome equilibrium between the two.[7]

When the demand for equality causes the renunciation of capable leadership and the elimination of distinctions based on merit, ability, and achievement, it places a premium on mediocrity. Liberty and equality cannot be worshipped as noble absolutes, and there are limits beyond which both ideals are incompatible with democracy. Democracy is a form of government which grants *political* equality to men as citizens, but it does not guarantee social and economic equality as well. It is true that democracy is threatened when men feel that the social order denies them opportunity, but opportunity is not the same as equality. If democracy cannot suppress social classes, it can diminish the exploitation of one class or group by another. If democracy cannot abolish differences in wealth, it can at least mitigate them and assure to all its citizens a reasonable standard of living and a certain measure of security. It extends to citizens with different talents and intelligence and different functions and status in the community an equality of *political* rights. Democracy makes its leaders responsible for the way in which they conduct its affairs; and, being a *political* structure, is not wedded to any particular economic program.

DEMOCRACY AND MAJORITY RULE

Dictatorship as well as democracy is capable of receiving mass support, and hence democracy cannot be adequately defined as "the will of the masses" or majority rule. Democracy accepts the majority principle and assumes an agreement or obligation of all to abide by the majority decision. On the other hand, it also seeks to reconcile the *volonté générale* with an equally basic democratic premise which guarantees fundamental rights to the individual. This conception of democracy has been criticized on the ground that it introduces a discussion of values into the discussion of democracy. It is argued that democracy is a form of government which in prac-

7. *The Crisis of Democracy,* pp. 24–26. See also Yves Simon, *Philosophy of Democratic Government* (Chicago, 1951), pp. 195–259.

tice is carried on according to the will of a majority of the electorate and that when there are limits to a majority's rule then some other group outside the majority has to determine the method of defining these limits which means in practice minority rule. If there is a criterion superior to the majority will, then the question arises as to who the final judge is and how this will is to be applied. Although it is recognized that certain freedoms are necessary as a means for obtaining majority decisions, it is sometimes argued that neither individuals nor minorities possess inalienable rights in a democracy because an existing majority can always decide to destroy them.[8]

Even if democracy were defined as majority rule, the consideration of values is not thereby excluded from rational political discussion. As Professor Francis W. Coker has pointed out, "There are different kinds of majority rule, and a desire for one kind does not commit anybody to a desire for another kind." [9] Both Plato and Aristotle distinguished between a "pure" democracy, in which the majority governed in the interest of all the people and in accordance with traditional customs or unwritten laws of the community, and a "corrupt" democracy, in which the majority ruled in its own interest and without regard for these higher obligations.[10] Similar evaluations which place limitations upon majority rule appear in many later classical statements of political theory, in the theoretical systems of both Locke and Jefferson, and in most other systematic discussions of democracy.[11]

It is sometimes contended even by the defenders of democracy that the will of the majority has the right to prevail because the greater number is also the more powerful physically. If resort were had to force, the superior strength of the majority would be sufficient to compel the minority to yield. From this point of view, democracy is a device which permits the minority to submit peace-

8. Willmoore Kendall, *John Locke and the Doctrine of Majority-Rule* (Urbana, 1941); by the same author, "Prolegomena to any Future Work on Majority Rule," *Journal of Politics,* XII (November, 1950), 694–713. For a criticism of Kendall and other "majority-rule democrats," see Francis W. Coker, "Some Present-Day Critics of Liberalism," *The American Political Science Review,* XLVII (March, 1953), 1–27; Herbert McClosky, "The Fallacy of Absolute Majority Rule," *The Journal of Politics,* XI (November, 1949), 637–654.

9. "Some Present-Day Critics of Liberalism," *op. cit.,* p. 9.

10. Aristotle, *Politics,* Bk. III, Chs. iv, vi, xi; Bk. IV, Chs. i, iv, xi, xiv; Bk. V, Ch. ix; Plato, *The Laws,* IV, 715.

11. For a discussion see Edwin Mims, Jr., *The Majority of the People* (New York, 1941).

fully and ultimately rests on force. "It is better to resort to counting heads instead of breaking them." Actually a government based merely upon force and possessing unlimited authority is not a democracy. This is because such a government by virtue of its majority support could prohibit the formation of an opposition, forbid those who disagree to speak and publish, and create and maintain popular support through the monopolistic manipulation of the press and radio. It would be ridiculous to argue that Germany would have been a democracy if the Nazis, instead of receiving thirty-three per cent of the votes in 1932, had attained fifty-one per cent. It is equally absurd to contend that Soviet Russia or Fascist Italy are examples of democracy because their governments attained huge majorities in popular elections.

Democracy accepts the majority principle, but it also assumes that the will of the majority will be accepted as the will of the whole community. An enthroned majority which is intolerant of minority opinion and which assumes the right to rule just because it is a majority does not provide the necessary integrating force in society upon which democracy depends. Although decisions must ultimately be reached through majority vote, they are taken only after a discussion in which the minority has had a chance to criticize the government. In the course of the debate each side learns from the other. By engaging in discussion with the minority the will of the majority ceases to be merely the formal will of a mathematical majority and assumes a more general and universal character which does justice to the whole community. This is because the ideas of the majority are widened to include those ideas of the minority which have established their truth in the debate and also because the views of the minority have also become broadened to include some ideas of the majority. Under these circumstances the majority is in the end permitted to have its way, but the decision has been reached through compromise and the minority has played an important role. Although discussion under these circumstances does not produce unanimity, it does provide a decision more broadly based and a greater degree of common consent. When majority rule is combined with an agreement to differ and with the principle of compromise, there can be no tyranny of the majority. The minority has not been totally ineffective, is more inclined to accept the majority decision, and does not pursue a policy of obstruction. On the other hand, the majority tolerates the existence of opposition and even makes concessions to its position. When a political party believes itself to be the sole possessor of an exclusive truth and as a result becomes intolerant of opposition, democracy breaks down. Government by discussion assumes that no party has a monopoly of the truth and seeks to reconcile and compromise the different viewpoints.

It must be admitted that these conditions are not present in all countries and that parliamentary institutions are operating in many countries which have not yet established the political morality or the system of ethics upon which democracy depends. Although interest has been focused generally upon institutions and the legal relationships between the various organs of government, the limitations upon which democracy depends must be self-imposed. No system of constitutional law can prevent an intolerant majority determined upon stripping the minority of its rights from doing so, and no amount of legal drafting can guarantee the observance of rules whereby discussion takes place in the spirit of moderation and of compromise. However, when discussion degenerates into a civil war of opinion and when the opposing forces reject the possibility of compromise, the very purpose of discussion has been destroyed. In the clash of extremes democracy can find no place, and the outcome is likely to be the victory of fascism or of left-wing totalitarianism based upon force.

Modern democracy began as a protest against class government and sought to curb the overbearing arrogance of a ruling class by transfering authority to the whole body of a nation. In the course of the struggle against class rule the contrast was drawn between the enfranchised classes and "the people" who constituted the more numerous unenfranchised mass outside of the government. However, those who thus idealized "the masses" did not mean to represent them as a class which was entitled to predominate and to be the sole exponent of the public will merely because it was the most numerous. Instead they thought of popular rule as the antithesis of class rule. They had in their immediate background the experience of a small privileged class which had abused its authority to the disadvantage of the whole community. They sought to transfer political power to all classes because they thought "the people" would think in terms of the national welfare rather than in terms of narrow class interests. Moreover, the participation of all classes would give unity and strength to the nation as a whole because each class would make its own contribution. In any case, it did not occur to them that a single class which constituted a majority of the whole might in the course of time become possessed with a self-regarding spirit and seek to capture control of the state to the exclusion of all other classes. Their view was that popular rule would have an integrating effect and that class antagonisms would disappear.

Although this view may be considered too optimistic, it does explain why democracy cannot be considered as merely "the rule of the masses." Such a conception conveys the idea of a division of the community into two opposing classes. There is the élite on the one hand and the undifferentiated multitude on the other. This idea, which is so inconsistent with the genius of democracy, is characteristic of undemocratic class-bound societies. The expression was in regular use in Germany and Russia and is still current in the less democratic countries. It is well known that Karl Marx's thought, born under a system of absolutism and habituated to German oligarchical conditions, emphasized a kind of reversed class rule with the "proletariat" on top. In the early days of the American republic the thinking of the Founding Fathers was still largely oligarchical, and hence democracy was commonly referred to as "the rule of the masses," a government of the "inferior" or vulgar conducted at the expense of the few. However, as democratic sentiment increased this idea was replaced by a faith in "the common man" and in "the people" generally who, by preventing the encroachments and aggressions of particular private interests, would promote the common good. Professor Carl Friedrich says that one of the difficulties confronting parliamentary democracy on the continent of Europe, where Rousseau's theory of the general will has found acceptance, is to provide the proper balance between majority rule and minority rights. He says that a tradition of radical majoritarianism, combined with a general skepticism about the capacity of man to free himself from the prejudice of class and economic interests, have given rise to the view that the majority has an indubitable "legitimacy" in the determination of public policy and general laws. The result is that political decisions are frequently viewed as an act of will rather than a matter for rational determination. Under these circumstances the rights of small minorities are likely to be suppressed through the paraphernalia of democratic procedure or else a recalcitrant minority, fearing that its rights will be voted away, will prevent the majority from acting. In the English-speaking world there has been a tendency to put the individual first and to guarantee his liberties even against the government; but Continental European democrats, in the tradition of the Jacobins, have tended to neglect these problems, to place a stronger emphasis upon the collective aspects of society and government, and to have less confidence in the capacity of the common man to deal with matters of common concern.[12]

DEMOCRACY AND PLANNING

One of the great controversies of our time centers around the extent to which economic planning is compatible with democracy. Some writers tend to link constitutional democracy with free enterprise and a free-market economy and believe that governmental planning requires a totalitarian system of government.[13] Others are inclined to feel that society must either plan or doom itself to a horrible chaos and speak of "planning for freedom" and the brave new world planning will secure.[14] Some advocates argue that planning requires governmental ownership of the means of production, while others say that governmental control over the operation of facilities is all that is necessary.[15] Still others argue that in no country is planning entirely absent or complete and that the issue is not "plan

12. Carl J. Friedrich, "The Political Theory of the New Democratic Constitutions," in Arnold J. Zurcher (ed.), *Constitutions and Constitutional Trends Since World War II* (New York, 1951), pp. 19–20, 33–34. "Nowhere on the Continent is there to be found any genuine 'belief in the common man,' as that belief is taken for granted in the United States. . . . Somehow, this lacuna in European democratic thought seems related to the exaggeration of the majority's views on one side and to the role of the state on the other." *Ibid.*, p. 33. See also by the same author, *The New Belief in the Common Man* (Boston, 1942), esp. pp. 121–150; Guglielmo Ferrero, *The Principles of Power* (New York, 1942), esp. pp. 174–186; Yves Simon, "The Doctrinal Issue Between the Church and Democracy," in Waldemar Gurian and M. A. Fitzsimons (eds.), *The Catholic Church in World Affairs* (Notre Dame, 1954), pp. 87–114 and *Philosophy of Democratic Government* (Chicago, 1951).

13. Friedrich Hayek, *The Road to Serfdom* (Chicago, 1944); John Jewkes, *Ordeal by Planning* (London, 1948).

14. Karl Mannheim, *Freedom, Power, and Democratic Planning* (New York, 1950).

15. For the two points of view see G. D. H. Cole, *Plan for Democratic Britain* (London, 1939), esp. pp. 35–40; and Barbara Wootton, *Freedom Under Planning* (Chapel Hill, 1949), esp. p. 11, where a distinction is made between planning with and without governmental ownership.

or no plan" but rather how much and what sort of planning can be attempted in a democracy.[16]

A part of this confusion can be explained as a misunderstanding over the meaning of terms. Neither the advocates nor the opponents of planning agree upon their definitions with the result that different authors are talking about different things. For example, much of the discussion of planning has been linked to socialism in spite of the fact that in neither theory nor practice is there any necessary relationship. It is possible for a country to nationalize its railroads and other utilities without giving any thought to planning; and it is possible to engage in extensive planning, as the United States did in World War II, without involving socialization at all. However, both advocates as well as opponents of planning frequently fail to make this distinction. This is understandable, even though the effect is to complicate a fruitful discussion of the planning issue, because socialist ideology has always stressed its interest in a planned economy and because the Soviet Union which is represented as a "socialist state" has engaged in large-scale planning.

There is no question that a fully planned and centrally directed economy involving complete socialization and the type of detailed planning practiced in the Soviet Union is incompatible with democracy. This is because the degree of control is too penetrating bringing about too great a concentration of power at the center. If ultimate decisions are made by a State Planning Commission armed with coercive powers, then the power of government has been extended into every aspect of life. With a vast increase in the powers of the executive and with the creation of a multitude of boards, commissions, and managerial positions, there arises the corresponding increase in the problem of making government responsive to the will of the people. Yet the role of the legislature would be greatly diminished because the work of planning involves the use of experts and cannot be done by legislation.

Even if free elections were permitted, the new power that full socialization inevitably puts into the hands of the government would empty these rights of any real meaning. It is plain enough that the power of big business and high finance is frequently a dan-

16. The literature in this field is tremendous. However, the reader will find Joseph A. Schumpeter, *Capitalism, Socialism and Democracy* (Second edition; New York, 1947), Pt. IV, particularly valuable as a general reference.

ger to the community; but if the authority now dispersed were concentrated at the center with both political and economic power
combined in the hands of a single group, then the people could be
manipulated so that their right to vote would become an empty
privilege. Moreover, economic decisions are not easily determined
by votes. It is impossible for the people to determine how many
automobiles should be produced in a single year, where a new plant
should be located, or at what price a pair of shoes should be sold.
Those who are most critical of the abuses of private power frequently overlook the dangers inherent in public power because they
assume that it will be exercised in a responsible manner.

With complete socialization the government becomes the sole
employer. The directors of economic organizations and trade union
officials become agents of the government; and since they are dependent upon the favor of government for their status, power, and
influence, they will administer their policies accordingly. Each individual is likely to be more sensitive to governmental pressure because if he falls out of favor there is nowhere else to go. In such a
society there is likely to be an emphasis on conformity and a penalty
for dissent; for there is only one road to power and social position
and that is through government service. Under these circumstances
it is difficult to see how an effective opposition could develop and
how the will of the people could prevail against the pressures of
government. As a matter of fact, elections would most probably
become the peaceful affairs that they are in the Soviet Union at the
present time with only one candidate in each district. Mere elections
are no safeguard to democracy unless conditions are present for the
maintenance and development of a critical public opinion.

Although private power is easily abused, the question really is
whether an omnipotent government can be held responsible. If public power is not made responsible to public opinion, it is even more
tyrannous and equally capable of abuse. There is every reason to
believe that, even though democratic ideas prevailed at first, total
planning would involve a way of life and habits of association in
which liberty could not endure against a kind of creeping totalitarianism which would gradually spread itself over all aspects of
human life. In any case, the burden falls on the advocates of total
planning to explain how these dangers can be met.

There is, of course, no reason why planning must be conceived of in these absolute terms. The nature of our society today requires the use of all available knowledge in the development of policies; and every modern government is learning better how to gather facts, to utilize the knowledge of experts so that scientific insight is brought to bear upon the solution of problems, and to plan a portion of its economic life. In the United States the government cannot avoid planning its defense policies, and basic decisions on these matters have an increasing effect upon the economy as a whole. Every democratic government in the world today has enacted legislation designed to control the deficiencies and abuses in a market economy and introduced a certain measure of planning to provide a more equitable distribution of wealth, reduce unemployment, and eliminate the exploitation of one individual by another.

The means used vary considerably from country to country. All governments have attempted through the control of money and credit systems to channel economic activity into directions calculated to promote social needs, and the regulation of basic industries, including the nationalization of important sectors in the economy, is now practiced in most democratic states. There is no doubt that partial planning in a mixed economy, where there is not a monopoly of power which a socialist economy inevitably entails, may be accomplished by democratic means. The experience of Great Britain since 1945 appears to indicate that democracy permits a great deal of economic planning even along socialist lines. However, even in that country it is well understood that total planning involves totalitarian politics and that the degree to which economic planning is possible depends upon the ability of government to secure an agreement upon objectives so as to provide widespread consent.[17]

Although the immediate trend in Europe at the end of the war in 1945 was toward socialization and planning, there has since been a growing realization that there are dangers in the extremes of either

17. For example, *The New Statesman and Nation,* November 6, 1948, p. 391, says that the democratic socialist "does not accept the Communist view that the State should plan in detail all production and distribution. It is not our aim either to compel everyone to do the work we think he is best suited to, or to provide people with goods according to our definition of their needs. Under proper safeguards, most people prefer to sell their labour and to buy their goods in a free market. What the democratic Socialist is determined to achieve is that the freedom of the market is a genuine freedom, and this demands interference with the price system at many points." See also Francis Williams, *Socialist Britain* (New York, 1949), pp. 85–110.

too much or too little government. In Great Britain, where the Bank of England and "key industries," such as the railroads, coal, electricity, gas, and civil aviation, have been nationalized, the operation of these industries under state ownership has not been as successful as many had hoped.[18] British experience appears to indicate that considerable nationalization is possible without causing any detriment to democratic processes. On the other hand, it also points up the dangers inherent in socialist planning. Even though eighty per cent of British industry remains in private hands, the problems connected with administration of the nationalized sector are enormous.

Laying aside the exaggerated claims on both sides of the controversy, it would appear that the friends of planning have demonstrated that under modern conditions an unplanned economy produces undesirable results and that partial planning involving a limited amount of socialization can be accomplished without sacrificing democratic procedures. On the other hand, the enemies of planning point to the dangers inherent in a planned economy and argue that it involves "the road to serfdom." Although it may be conceded that planning need not be the road to serfdom and that the real question confronting democracies has to do with how much and what type of planning is consistent with democratic procedures, the supporters of planning still need to give a great deal more constructive thought to the manner in which planning can be fitted into the processes of constitutional government.[19] There is a great deal of difference between the welfare state and a socialist state. It is one thing for the government to foster the health, security, and well-being of the people and still another for it to take over and operate all the industries in the country. In the absence of necessity demonstrated by facts it would appear to be desirable to avoid the dangers inherent in nationalization. It is to be hoped that an increased knowledge of how to handle the social and economic mechanism and how to use technicians without turning the formation of policy over to bureaucrats will make it possible to build administrative

18. See Eugene O. Golob, *The Isms: A History and Evaluation* (New York, 1954), pp. 284–310; Robert A. Brady, *Crisis in Britain* (Berkeley, 1950). For a discussion of economic planning in France and Italy, see Mario Einaudi, Maurice Byé, and Ernesto Rossi, *Nationalization in France and Italy* (Ithaca, 1955).

19. For an outstanding contribution on this subject, see Robert A. Dahl and Charles E. Lindbloom, *Politics, Economics, and Welfare* (New York, 1953).

controls and yet safeguard enough liberty and enterprise so that initiative is maintained.

*   *   *   *   *   *

A full account of the theory of democracy is outside the scope of this book. As a matter of fact, it is impossible to discuss fully the bare essentials and their necessary implications. In the following chapter a few suggestions are made concerning the preservation of democracy; but the preceding discussion, which has focused mainly upon a few key issues, indicates that a better knowledge of the nature of democracy is important if it is to be preserved.

Chapter 10

The Future of Democracy

In no country do democratic institutions operate as smoothly as they once did. This is because we live in an age of economic crisis and international tension necessitating the exercise of governmental powers not warranted by traditional conceptions of authority. Even in countries where democratic constitutions appear to be established firmly the people have become increasingly acquainted with various kinds of "crisis" and "emergency" regimes. More and more temporary expedients designed for extraordinary situations have become a part of the regular procedure. In Great Britain the national government of Ramsay MacDonald demanded and received from the House of Commons authority to legislate by order-in-council to reduce expenditures. Thus the House of Commons under the threat of financial crisis abdicated its historic role as custodian of the purse and granted temporarily to the cabinet dictatorial powers in public finance. Although it may be argued that the MacDonald government had a majority which approved these measures and that a vote on the budget always involves a vote of confidence so that the cabinet could have undoubtedly secured their enactment without any change, still the fact remains that the regular procedure was not followed partially because of fear on the part of some government supporters that the issues would compromise them in the eyes of their constituents.

Since the cabinet was authorized to act by special decrees, the minority was also denied an adequate opportunity to criticize and discuss the government's policies.[1]

Under the Third French Republic the practice had grown up of voting "full powers" to the ministry permitting it to legislate by decree. This was the expedient used by Raymond Poincaré in 1926 in order to stabilize the French currency. In the years that followed there was an increasing tendency for ministries when faced with critical domestic or foreign difficulties to ask the Parliament to abdicate its normal functions and hand over decree powers to the executive. As a matter of fact, the cleavages among the parties were so great and the political situation so unstable that the issuance of "decree laws," subject only to later parliamentary ratification, became after 1934 the regular and normal procedure.[2] Although it would be an exaggeration to say that the reliance on delegated emergency powers caused the swift collapse of France after the German invasion started, it may be taken as an indication that regular parliamentary government had already broken down.

Before World War II the use of emergency powers had become widespread even in countries, such as Belgium and Switzerland, which have thus far withstood the threat of dictatorship.[3] In times of crisis the time-consuming and cumbrous technique of parliamentary discussion and deliberation may appear ill-suited to the need for swift and efficient action. The necessity to resort to extraordinary procedures in these countries indicates quite clearly why the strain was too great in countries with less experience in constitutional government.

1. There were at this time other significant departures from the accepted ways of English government and politics. For example, there was the mysterious role played by the King in persuading MacDonald to head a coalition government, the independent actions of the Prime Minister in the formation of the cabinet, and a complete disregard for the party system. Members of the cabinet were permitted to oppose part of the government's program, and the Conservative party did not assume the role of leadership which under the circumstances it ordinarily would have done. See Clinton L. Rossiter, *Constitutional Dictatorship* (Princeton, 1948), pp. 177–183; Rogers, *Crisis Government*, pp. 76–86; Harold J. Laski, *The Crisis and the Constitution* (London, 1932).

2. For a discussion see Otto Kirchheimer, "Decree Powers and Constitutional Law in France under the Third Republic," *American Political Science Review*, XXXIV (December, 1940), 1104–23; André Géraud, *The Grave Diggers of France* (Garden City, New York, 1944); Rossiter, *op. cit.*, pp. 117–129.

3. Loewenstein, "Legislative and Executive Power," *op. cit.*, pp. 598–606.

EVALUATION OF PRESENT KNOWLEDGE

Modern totalitarianism is a reaction to the disintegration of society caused by contradictions inherent in liberal individualistic philosophy and calls into question many of the basic assumptions underlying the modern democratic state. Although the Nazis and Fascists were never able to win a majority in a free democratic election, both parties became important mass movements and attracted enough support to seize control of the state. They encountered fairly weak and mild resistance because there were relatively few who were opposed to them and who were at the same time sufficiently attached to the old regime to put up a vigorous defense against its enemies. Emphasis in this study has been placed upon the reasons why these totalitarian movements were successful, why they received the support that they did, and why it was that so large a percentage of the population was willing to abandon democratic institutions. However, in spite of all the work that has been devoted to the subject, there is still no definitive explanation for the rise of modern dictatorships. As Reinhold Niebuhr, a distinguished Protestant theologian, has said,

> Whenever modern idealists are confronted with the divisive and corrosive effects of man's self-love, they look for some immediate cause of this perennial tendency, usually in some specific form of social organization. One school holds that men would be good if only political institutions would not corrupt them; another believes that they would be good if the prior evil of a faulty economic organization could be eliminated. Or another school thinks of this evil as no more than ignorance, and therefore waits for a more perfect educational process to redeem man from his partial and particular loyalties. But no school asks how it is that an essentially good man could have produced corrupting and tyrannical political organizations or exploiting economic organizations, or fanatical and superstitious religious organizations.[4]

If the conclusions reached in the preceding chapters are sound, dictatorship is the result of an intrinsic weakness of contemporary democracy which is partly institutional but which is mainly psychological and moral. The failure of democratic leadership to muster necessary electoral and legislative support made it impossible for the executive to mobilize the power of the state or to de-

4. *The Children of Light and the Children of Darkness* (New York, 1947), p. 17.

velop and fulfill any broad public policy; and this crisis in authority in turn brought democratic government into contempt even among its supporters and had the effect of strengthening the antidemocratic elements in society. The contemporary crisis of democracy, therefore, is mainly spiritual and psychological. Its roots must be found in the loss of a common unity, in the inability of parties and interest groups to achieve agreement on fundamental common aims, and in their failure to find and accept a common moral purpose. As Waldemar Gurian has said,

> Totalitarian religions are attempts to unify for action a society not fully developed—as in Russia; or a society that is disintegrating because of the uncompromising conflicts of different groups—as in Germany; or because of a passive skepticism—as in Italy, which was not willing to oppose an apparently vitalistic dynamism. This external unification can result in spectacular successes. But it remains an external one. It does not create new life. It effects advances from a backward state, or a concentration of power. I think that as tyrannical military monarchs in the Hellenistic period were proofs of the exhaustion of the Greek world, totalitarianism in countries with an advanced civilization must be regarded not as a symptom of strength, but of weakness. External stimuli are necessary where spontaneous actions are no longer possible.[5]

Much of the writing about dictatorships involves the use of abstractions which have a certain utility if not pushed too far and if not presented with an air of dogmatic confidence. For example, those who argue that fascism was the revolt of the lower middle classes do not mean to imply that there were no other groups attracted to the movement or that all members of the middle class were its supporters. Such a concept is merely a convenient abstraction, and the question arises as to whether and to what extent it is a useful one. Behind the mass calculations and vast abstractions there are always real men and women who are suffering and hoping and individual families who have a stake in what happens. The analysis given here suggests that a better understanding would be achieved by abandoning many of these generalizations and giving instead a faithful account of what actually happened. It is only in this way that one can learn the complexity of human motivation, the variety of factors which must be fitted together to "explain" political movements, and the reasons why events in one country

5. "The Rise of Totalitarianism in Europe," *Annual Report of the American Historical Association,* III (1942), 303–304.

are not duplicated in another. There are those who will say that it is impossible to study politics in this manner and there are many more who will remain satisfied with the *cliché* or a slogan. However, such an attitude does not increase our knowledge of political movements and merely multiplies the present confusion. There is no doubt that a more precise and a more accurate account can be given than has even been attempted by many authors; and it is only on the basis of such a background that an intelligent appraisal and understanding of dictatorships can be made.

Many scholars become preoccupied with the brutality, cruelty, and bloodshed under dictatorships in an effort to show that fascism is a malicious outbreak of barbarity and brutality. For example, more than two-thirds of Hannah Arendt's book entitled *The Origins of Totalitarianism* is devoted to a discussion of anti-semitism and imperialism.[6] Anti-semitism, the use of torture, and the ruthless treatment of minorities are certainly abominable features of these regimes, but a discussion of this kind does not tell us much about the causes of dictatorships. Although these facts are sufficient cause to condemn totalitarianism in its entirety, they do not in themselves explain the reasons why people at this particular time in history should turn their backs once again to democracy and support a different kind of regime. It may be argued that brutality and cruelty are only symptoms; that fascism is a revolution which, like all revolutions, releases ferocious instincts in man; and that these features have been characteristic of all revolutions from the beginning of time.[7] The French Revolution marked a period

6. New York, 1951. The first 300 pages in a 439-page book deal with these two subjects but the entire volume is devoted to a discussion of the use of terror, oppression, and vicious cruelty.

7. Professor F. A. Hermens, *The Tyrants' War and the People's Peace* (Chicago, 1944), pp. 132–133, has pointed out an additional reason: "We must bear in mind that tyranny develops out of party fights within a democracy, which lead to near-anarchy; that one of the parties, with the 'tyrant' as its leader, takes over all the power for itself at a time when the people are tired of disorder; and that this party must establish an especially tyrannical rule because it was preceded by a democracy. In view of their democratic experience, people are more intensely aware of what goes on in politics than they would be, for example, under an absolute monarchy; and, since so many more of them take an active interest in politics, a large number have to be forcibly overcome. *Tyrannical pressure from above is so great, therefore, because it has to suppress so much democratic pressure from below.*" (Italics added). See also pp. 129–150 for an interesting comparison of Plato's description of tyranny with actual political conditions prior to the rise of dictatorship in Europe.

of intolerance, fanaticism, brutality, and vicious oppression which is comparable to the present day. Any modern conservative will emotionally agree with Edmund Burke, when he commented on the utter destruction of the French Revolution, the seizure of the king and queen, and how mob rule had replaced a regime which had stood for centuries.[8]

Many leftist writers have professed to find fascist tendencies in the United States. The burden of their argument appears to be that those who do not agree with them or who are not at least somewhat "progressive" are "fascist" or have "fascist tendencies." Since they consider fascism to be a conservative and nationalist movement, American politicians who fit into that category represent a clear and present danger.[9] Other writers present a more refined and scholarly approach but arrive at the same conclusions. It is contended, for example, that monopoly capitalism leads to fascism, and the concentration of economic power in America is presented as frantic proof that the United States is headed for the American equivalent of fascism.[10] It is clear from what has been said that such statements are derived from a preconceived philosophy of history, that they are based upon a superficial, rather than a thorough, knowledge of totalitarian movements, and that an analogy of this kind ignores the power of tradition and the importance of special conditions peculiar to the United States. The fact that American political institutions have been reasonably successful in their operation, whereas those of Germany and Italy were not, seems to have been largely ignored.

The truth is that democracy has failed where it did not produce satisfactory results. Of all forms of government democracy is the most delicate requiring a long period for maturation and growth

8. See his *Reflections on the French Revolution* (Everyman's Library; New York, 1910), esp. p. 77 et seq.

9. For a discussion see H. Arthur Steiner, "Fascism in America?" *The American Political Science Review,* XXIX (1935), 821–830. The reader has undoubtedly seen many more recent articles which take such an assumption as their starting point.

10. Brady, *Business as a System of Power,* cited *supra.* The force of this argument is not altered by the *bon mot* to the effect that "if America ever becomes fascist she will call it something else." The same type of deterministic reasoning, but from an opposing point of view, can be found in Hayek, *The Road to Serfdom,* previously cited, which takes as its theme that planning leads to fascism, and John T. Flynn, *As We Go Marching* (New York, 1944), which argues that deficit spending leads to militarism, an aggressive foreign policy, and finally to fascism.

and presupposing the inculcation of an appropriate philosophy without which it cannot withstand the forces of disruption. When the pressures impinging on the government's stability are moderate, it can adjust to them and undergo gradual reformation or evolution; but when they are extreme, the desperate civil conflict generally culminates in the elevation of a tyrant.

The "best form of government," as Aristotle said, is relative to circumstances. Under right conditions and favorable circumstances democracy undoubtedly is the best form of government and secures the most satisfactory results.[11] However, when these conditions are not present, democracy may at the same time be one of the worst kinds of government. It is sometimes forgotten that the judgment of both Plato and Aristotle was against democracy; and although they were unfamiliar with modern "representative democracy," the reasons for their adverse judgment and the circumstances out of which it arose may be instructive to us at the present time.

At no time has democracy been widely adopted in practice nor is it likely to be in the future. History does not teach us that men really wish to govern themselves but that they want to be well governed and expect results from the government in power. An ardent Nazi probably had no more objection to following Hitler than an English Conservative had in following Sir Winston Churchill. Moreover, the leader was not conceived of as the absolute antithesis of democracy but as a channel of the people's thoughts and actions. Instead of the people themselves seeking the truth through the organs and institutions of discussion, they sought to find it through the eyes of a "chosen leader" who supposedly possessed a higher vision. Fascism grew out of democracy, and a better understanding of the factors responsible for its success may lead to more knowledge concerning the conditions necessary for the operation of democracy and the manner in which it may best be preserved. In any case, not all nations are capable of operating

11. See the interesting study of Edward P. Cheyney, "Historical Tests of Democracy," in *Law in History and Other Essays* (New York, 1927), pp. 90–129, in which the author has made a comparative study of the results of three main periods of English history: 1600 to 1618, representing autocratic government; 1800 to 1818, representing aristocracy; and 1900 to 1918, representing liberal democracy. His conclusion is that democracy has produced "more wise legislation and administration than any other form of government."

a democratic government. A foreign policy which ignores this fact must either resort to the subterfuge followed during the last war when allied propaganda referred to all of our allies, including the Soviet Union, as "democracies," or else fail because it does not receive the support it otherwise could secure.

OUTLOOK IN EUROPE

Unfortunately parliamentary government today must be carried on in the countries where it has been re-established under conditions unfavorable to democracy. In every one of these countries there are staggering problems of economic reconstruction, constant tensions resulting from the threat of war, a divided and confused citizenry, and a basic disagreement on fundamental matters. Although the new constitutions contain few new ideas, their framers made an effort to avoid past mistakes and added provisions designed to provide a greater mechanical stability for the executive.[12] In the French, Italian, and West German constitutions there are clauses which require a special procedure for placing on the agenda motions critical of the cabinet and likely to bring about its downfall, which delay the voting upon such motions in order to avoid the fall of a ministry on a "snap vote," which require extraordinary affirmative majorities for the adoption of a vote of no-confidence, and which seek to curb reckless opposition by granting to the government the power of dissolution.

In neither France nor Italy have these efforts to provide an artificial stability to the executive proved successful. In both countries the government is weak and divided, there is a strong Communist party, and a slight shift of the vote can bring down a government. The average life of a French cabinet under the Fourth Republic has been about six months, and there has been a tendency for the period of time needed to put together a new cabinet to increase. Although the post-war record of Italian cabinets appears to be much better than that of France, this is only because the Christian

---

12. For a discussion see Arnold J. Zurcher (ed.), *Constitutions and Constitutional Trends Since World War II* (New York, 1951). On page 199 Professor Karl Loewenstein says: "The expectation that the nations liberated from Nazi-fascist despotism would return to their constitutions with jubilation did not materialize. Return they did. What else could they do? But it was a far cry from the democratic *élan* the preceding generations had exhibited. . . . The business of constitution-making was attended to dutifully and without enthusiasm."

Democrats won a majority of the seats in the Chamber of Deputies in 1948. Since this was the first time that a single political party ever secured a majority in Italy and since the election was held under abnormal circumstances, it may be assumed that this is not likely to happen again. In any case, the results of the 1953 election were very disappointing to the Christian Democrats, and events since that time indicate that the political situation in that country is likely to remain unsettled for some time.

The French National Assembly, which is now split into six major political divisions, frequently seems incapable of action. For example, since the liberation it has been unable to adopt a budget in advance of the year to which it applies and has been either unable or unwilling to solve the problems of stabilization and expansion of the French economy. All of the major parties, with the exception of the Communists, have divisions within their own ranks. As a matter of fact, one of the curious things about contemporary French politics is that party discipline has become more relaxed in spite of an electoral system specially designed to promote party regularity and that the free-and-easy system of the Third Republic which permitted deputies to "shop around" from one group to another and to vote their own opinions is increasingly becoming a feature of French political life. *Plus ça change, plus c'est la même chose.* Moreover, the type of issues confronting the country at the present time, such as those involving Algeria, Indo-China, the European Army, European political unification, German rearmament, the French Union, and domestic social and economic policies, appears to be breaking the existing groups apart and hindering all efforts towards coalition. As a matter of fact, François Goguel in a recent book says that contemporary conditions in France differ from those under the Third Republic when a coalition of left-center or right-center parties could cohere reasonably well in that a different majority in the Assembly is needed to support every major policy presented by the government.[13]

Although Italy made astonishing progress along the path of free democracy after her emergence from fascism, the political situation has recently deteriorated to the point that the country is now faced with a parliamentary paralysis resembling that of France. In the first eight months after the parliamentary election held in June,

13. *France Under The Fourth Republic* (Ithaca, 1952), p. 138.

1953, five different men had already been entrusted with the task of forming a cabinet, and the country had been without a real cabinet during nearly half of this time. The governing coalition at the present time consists of the Christian Democrats, plus three minor groups—the Social Democrats, Liberals, and Republicans. Since both the Right and the Left made important gains in the 1953 election, these parties have a majority in the Chamber of only 16 votes. This combination can be held together only with great difficulty because of the temperamental character and intense rivalries of the minor party leaders and because of dissensions within the Christian Democratic party itself. Under these circumstances the government is necessarily weak and hampered in its efforts to deal with basic problems confronting the country. The minor parties which lost votes in the last election are divided on the policies they ought to pursue in order to win back their supporters. The result has been that fragments have been chipped off both sides of the Center bloc.

It is impossible to make an accurate generalization about conditions in Germany. The country is still under occupation; its politics could hardly be said to have crystallized into anything resembling a definite pattern; and although Dr. Konrad Adenauer's Christian Democrats won a majority in the last election, it is doubtful that this is likely to be an ordinary recurrence. The Bonn Constitution has gone further than the new constitutions in France and Italy in attempting to avoid frequent cabinet crises. The Chancellor has emerged as the "strong man" who appoints and dismisses the other ministers and who may even keep them in office in the face of parliamentary disapproval since there is no provision for voting no-confidence in ministers. Although a Chancellor is not officially appointed until after he has secured the approval of a majority in the Bundestag, he cannot easily be gotten rid of by Parliament.[14] A vote of no-confidence is ineffective unless a majority of the legal membership of the Bundestag simultaneously elects a successor to the chancellorship. Thus the opposition must agree on a new cabinet

14. If no Chancellor is elected by a majority within 14 days, then a new ballot takes place in which the person receiving the greatest number of votes is elected. For a discussion see Hans Nawiasky, "Der Einfluss des Bundespraesidenten auf Bildung und Bestand der Bundesregierung," *Die Oeffentliche Verwaltung,* III (March, 1950), 161–163; Elmer Plischke, *The West German Federal Government* (Washington, 1952), pp. 82–86.

before the overthrow of an old one, and a Chancellor who has been elected at the beginning of the legislative period may be reasonably certain of staying in office for a full four-year term.

Opinion is divided as to how this new arrangement will operate under German conditions and how effective it will prove to be in the long run. Some observers are inclined to feel that a desire to avoid executive instability has caused the weight to shift too much to the executive side. For example, Karl Loewenstein calls it a "demo-authoritarian form of government" which in a country with weak democratic traditions might easily evolve into executive supremacy.[15] On the other hand, it must be admitted that it is a far more stable system than that of the Weimar Republic which had twenty cabinets between February, 1919, and January, 1933.

If the Bundestag refuses to pass a measure deemed vital by the government, the Chancellor can ask the President to declare a "state of legislative emergency." Decrees issued under these circumstances have the force of law providing that the Bundesrat (Federal Council) gives its consent. Although this provision is similar to Article 48 in the Weimar Constitution, an attempt has been made to reduce the danger by providing that emergency legislation must not amend or suspend any part of the Constitution, that the Bundesrat must agree, and that decree powers may be granted only once and for not more than a six-month period to an individual Chancellor during his term of office. As to how these provisions will work out in practice remains to be seen. Actual experience dates only from 1949, a period obviously too short to draw any valid conclusions. Up to now Chancellor Adenauer with the aid of an intrenched bureaucracy has ruled the country on a paternalistic pattern.

Representative institutions are the machinery set up to bring about compromises between competing interests in a state. Although the interests who have to lose may not be satisfied with the results, the machinery used under a constitutional system persuades them to consent to lose. Constitutional government breaks down when individuals or groups refuse peaceably to lose, for under these circumstances the dominant interest in the state establishes control

15. "The Government and Politics of Germany," in James T. Shotwell (ed.), *Governments of Continental Europe* (Revised edition; New York, 1952), pp. 574–580.

by force and governs by coercion rather than consent. Contemporary democracy is still confronted with the problem of how to create an executive strong enough to govern and thus give stability to the government and yet at the same time provide for democratic controls without creating the danger of obstruction. Therefore, the greatest danger to the future of democracy lies in the absence of an underlying agreement among social groups about the scope and purpose of government and its relation to society. Post-war parliamentary behavior in both France and Italy frequently reflects the serious divisions in the country, and the bitterness of feeling has often been manifested by actual physical combat among the deputies. The so-called "center groups" in both of these countries are greatly divided and constitute a "center" only because they occupy a position between extremes. In France political clericals, secular liberals, Marxian socialists, conservative agrarians, and pro-capitalist groups must subdue their differences in order to carry on the government and protect it against the opposing extremes. In Italy political opinion has tended to polarize into supporters of some form of Marxism and their opponents who have thus far voted mainly for the Christian Democratic party. However, the last election appears to indicate that many of those who supported Catholicism in the past may be more inclined to vote for a rightist group in the future.

In both France and Italy Communism appears to have attracted permanently the support of a large percentage of the voters.[16] However, far more dangerous than the size and strength of the Communist movement is the internal disunity of the non-Communist parties. Unlike the numerous but weak center parties in France, the Christian Democrats have a large following in Italy. However, the party is sharply divided within its own ranks, and a major reason for governmental instability in that country has been not only the failure of the party and its allies to win a majority in the last election but also the failure of various elements within the party to agree

16. See Mario Einaudi, Jean-Marie Domenach, and Aldo Garosci, *Communism in Western Europe* (Ithaca, 1951). The Italian Communist party is apparently better organized, better financed, and has more support than the French Communist party. However, there is little likelihood that Communism can win a majority at the polls in either country in the immediate future. For a more recent discussion of Italian Communism see the series of articles by C. L. Sulzberger in the *New York Times*, March 15, 16, 17, 1954.

upon a common policy which all members can accept.[17] The failure to achieve agreement among parties on any fundamental aims and their unwillingness to acknowledge that there are values upon which parties must agree make it impossible for the government to plan any long-term constructive action and compel ministers to utilize all their energies in trying merely to stay in office. Under these circumstances an atmosphere is likely to be created which is particularly favorable for the growth of extremist groups.

PRESERVATION OF DEMOCRACY

The greatest danger confronting European democracy is the lack of consensus; and a superficial examination of parliamentary conditions and of the increasing number of parties in post-war legislatures present a picture similar to the one which prevailed prior to the rise of fascism. However, there are also underlying factors which are not so readily discernible to the foreign observer but which may give parliamentary institutions a better chance for success. Although the fundamental causes for dictatorship are still not much understood and still provide a subject for bitter partisan discussions, it would be a mistake to conclude that those who have lived under totalitarianism learned nothing from the experience. In other words, democracy has undoubtedly gained in prestige as a reaction to the terrible past.

Emphasis has been placed upon political institutions, but institutions are merely the means to an end. When one speaks of democracy, he has in mind a form of government; but he also thinks in terms of certain values and a way of life. To provide an integrated philosophy of democracy and to explore the moral, political, and economic conditions for its preservation are beyond the scope of this book. It would be impossible, in any case, to chart a blueprint or construct an absolute formula; for the path to be followed must vary to some extent in accordance with tradition, geography, and the peculiar nature of conditions in the different countries. However, it may be appropriate to suggest here at least a few general principles which, although vague and in need of further development, would help stem the present crisis, restore

17. See Mario Einaudi and François Goguel, *Christian Democracy in Italy and France* (Notre Dame, 1952), pp. 66–74.

consensus, and replace the present notion of warring groups and classes with an integrating force in society.

1. Moral basis of democracy. In any stable political system there must be a set of beliefs and institutions which integrate and strengthen each other. Thus every form of government ultimately rests upon a philosophy containing certain assumptions or a common core of beliefs. A democratic system is based upon respect for the human personality and for the conscience and moral dignity of man. The Western world owes to Christianity belief in the brotherhood of man, the idea that each person has an immortal soul, and the notion that all persons are equal in the sight of God. "Democracy," as John Middleton Murry has said,

> is based not only in theory but in fact upon the reality of a universal obligation to obey the moral law. If that obligation is not recognized, and acted on, democracy must, in time of real stress, collapse. If the validity of the moral law is an illusion, so is the validity of democracy.[18]

Since democracy is based upon principles found in the Bible and teachings of the Church, it is sometimes argued that the preservation of democracy requires a return to religion. Such a development would undoubtedly be of great assistance, for there is considerable reason to question whether morals can in the long run be permanently divorced from religion. On the other hand, there are practical dangers in resting democracy too firmly on a Christian foundation. In the first place, Christianity was able to exist for many years without democracy and is compatible with other types of government. Moreover, even if the present trend towards secularism were reversed in the Western world, a Christian solution could be applied only to a minority of the world's population. India, Ceylon, Israel, and Turkey are now experimenting with democracy; and it would indeed be unfortunate if the political institutions in these countries were doomed to failure until Christianity had gained a considerable number of converts. Moreover, Christendom is divided into many branches and the fact that strongly held religious beliefs divide men into factions is frequently mentioned as an important reason for keeping democratic politics secular.[19] Finally, many of those who

18. "The Moral Foundations of Democracy," *Fortnightly*, CLXII (September, 1947), 168.
19. Oskar Bauhofer, "Democracy and the Catholic Church," in Waldemar

urge a return to religion do so, not out of personal conviction, but because they think it socially and politically useful. As H. B. Mayo has pointed out, "There hardly seems a shorter way of undermining religious beliefs than to urge their adoption not because they are believed to be true but because they are socially useful 'myths'— what Sorel called 'necessary impostures,' and Plato 'noble lies.' Such a movement violates all religious integrity and does dubious service to democracy." [20]

Although human liberty and the dignity of the human person are most secure on Christian grounds, a genuine democracy cannot impose on its citizens or demand from them any philosophic or any religious creed. St. Thomas Aquinas taught that morals may be discovered by reason and supported by natural law, and it may be argued that the same is true of government. Moreover, moral action is impossible without freedom of choice. On the other hand, it does not follow that all truth is relative, that the task of the politician is merely to follow opinion wherever it may lead, and that all principles may be compromised. One of the weaknesses of the liberal philosophy is its assumption that there are no final truths, that one opinion is as good as another, and that the individual has rights but no corresponding duties. Since it was assumed that the individual best served society by pursuing his own self-interest, the state was divided into warring groups and classes without any sense of community. After all, without some principles only force is left. This is why democratic politics cannot be defined as the science of "who gets what, when, how," [21] and why the task of the legislator cannot

Gurian and M. A. Fitzsimons (eds.), *The Catholic Church in World Affairs* (Notre Dame, 1954), p. 77: "Modern society is spiritually pluralistic, that is, lacking a basic spiritual unity of public import, such as was found in the Catholic faith in the Middle Ages. . . . It is clear that it is not now in the power of either the Church or the state to reverse the course of history, or even simply to ignore the spiritual 'pluralism' of modern society. This is not moral abdication, on the part of the Church. The Catholic Church continues to hold up to the modern mind the guiding principles of a truly Christian Society,—not in a romantic conservatism, as seduced by memories and claims of a past age, but in an essentially missionary spirit. . . . There are few countries in Continental Europe that are still open to a sort of formal co-partnership and avowed moral solidarity between Church and state." See also Jacques Maritan, *Man and the State* (Chicago, 1951), pp. 108–119.

20. H. B. Mayo, *Democracy and Marxism* (New York, 1955), p. 266.

21. The title of a book by Harold D. Lasswell published in 1936 by McGraw-Hill is *Politics: Who Gets What, When, How.* The author states (p. 3) that "the study of politics is the study of influence and the influential" and that "the influential are those who get the most of what there is to get."

be adequately described by reference to him as "a skilled compromiser," "a combiner of wills," or as merely a "broker" among competing interest groups. If our statesmen are unable to see the light and can only feel the heat when it is turned on by a powerful pressure group, then it is difficult to resist the logic of the Marxian or Fascist claim for the right of a minority to seize control of the state.[22] Government is not merely a reflection of what factions want and are able to get; but it exists, as Madison pointed out in the tenth number of the *Federalist,* to control the effects of factionalism. The political party, supported by an adequate electoral system, has as its end the task of uniting for political purposes conflicting individual and group interests; and the public interest ought not to be viewed as having no objective reality.

Although moral absolutes ought to be kept at a minimum, democracy places a high premium, not merely upon freedom, but also upon truth, honesty, and a high level of public morality. Any number of observers have given eloquent testimony to the failure of democracies because defenders possessed few principles and little faith in their own position.[23] This is particularly important when it is realized that communism is a movement determined on reaching its goal and that there are few problems confronting society for which it does not claim to have an answer.

2. Respect for tradition and authority. The atomistic conception of society, upon which liberalism erected its theory of the state, is in need of correction; for the state is not an artificial instrumentality based upon the claims of individuals but arises as a natural necessity out of man's social nature. Individuals do not create society but are born into it. Since every society has its roots in a particular historical tradition, one of the weaknesses of liberalism was its tendency to ignore these roots and exalt abstract reason to the neglect of custom and tradition. Edmund Burke was right in view-

22. The legislator, of course, must take into consideration the opinions of his constituents; but the idea that he merely records these views and that the politician is an unscrupulous person lacking in moral responsibility or the duty to exercise any leadership Yves Simon has correctly designated "the cab-driver theory of government." "The Doctrinal Issue Between the Church and Democracy," in Gurian and Fitzsimons, *op. cit.,* pp. 87–114; and *Philosophy of Democratic Government* (Chicago, 1951), pp. 146–155. See also John H. Hallowell, *The Moral Foundation of Democracy* (Chicago, 1953), pp. 54–63.

23. See John H. Hallowell, *The Decline of Liberalism as an Ideology* (Berkeley and Los Angeles, 1943).

ing society as the product of the "wisdom of ages"; and the truth of his criticisms of the French philosophers for believing that political institutions could be constructed *de novo* through the exercise of pure reason has been demonstrated by political events. "I cannot conceive," Burke wrote,

> how any man can have brought himself to that pitch of presumption, to consider his country as nothing but *carte blanche,* upon which he may scribble whatever he pleases. A man . . . may wish his society otherwise constituted than he finds it; but a good patriot, and a true politician, always considers how he shall make the most of the existing materials of his country. A disposition to preserve, and an ability to improve, taken together, would be my standard of a statesman.[24]

Burke's teaching differed from that of Rousseau in that it restricted the freedom of subjects to exercise their consent and limited the sovereign's right to exercise his power. A political theory of freedom, therefore, could never carry its conclusions to the point where it might destroy the framework of a civic tradition. One might say that Burke appealed from the spoken to the unspoken rules of freedom and asserted that the Jacobins in proceeding to a comprehensive destruction of the historic order unwittingly eliminated the very basis on which continuous social improvement could be made. The French Revolution, therefore, was the literal pursuit of sound political principles within a community not equipped with the traditional practice and wisdom through which these principles must be interpreted; for progress must rely on the existing society as its matrix and thereby testify to its own respect for tradition.

Throughout the nineteenth century Burke's admonitions remained largely fruitless; for it is the essence of tradition to remain unformulated and the Burkeian doctrine, in any case, could only prophesy the doom of communities not already blessed with a tradition of civic freedom. Moreover, liberalism appeared to have made great achievements in Europe well beyond the limits allowed by the prognosis implied in Burke's teaching. This was because the soil of Europe was not nearly so unprepared for freedom as might have appeared at the time when Burke wrote. After all, many ancient strains of freedom were delicately woven into the fabric of European culture. For example, religious freedom for Moham-

24. *Reflections on the French Revolution* (Everyman's Library; New York, 1910), p. 153.

medans and Jews was secure in the thirteenth century over important Mediterranean regions of Europe. Frederick II of Prussia established a considerable measure of religious tolerance; and although legal guarantees of freedom were incomplete during his rule, he did recognize the majesty of the law as superior to that of the king. Deriving guidance from these and other traditional strains, liberalism gradually spread into Europe after the French Revolution; and although most continental countries lacked a complete liberal tradition, the period from 1867 to 1914 witnessed the rise of free institutions, a gradual assuagement of the revolutionary spirit, and the apparent victory of civility all over Western and Central Europe.

Although the rapid succession of regimes in France seemed to justify many of Burke's criticisms, it was not until the end of World War I that the prophecy flowing from his teachings began to be fulfilled. An excess of theoretical aspirations over practical wisdom, which was even more extravagant than in eighteenth century France, had arisen in Russia; and in the years that followed Russian totalitarianism gained followers throughout Europe in sufficient numbers to disrupt civic concord and imperil freedom even in countries which had already passed the danger zone of liberal transformation. "The heritage of Jacobinism continued to alienate European intellectuals from the existing social order and to fix their aspirations on a comprehensive reconstruction of society to be achieved by a violent upheaval." [25] Thus freedom was eventually destroyed in Italy, Germany, Austria, and other European states by a fascist counter-revolution which had armed itself with the nihilism of its communist opponents.

Professor Boris Mirkine-Guetzévitch has shown how the defiance of national habit in constitutions created after 1919 contributed to the weakness of democratic states.[26] The experts in public law who framed these documents were motivated by high standards of professional excellence; but they provided a slavish imitation of British and other parliamentary models and defined the processes of popular government according to abstract principles. The result was that these constitutions jeopardized the future stability of popular government because by failing to reflect national

25. Michael Polanyi, "On Liberalism and Liberty," *Encounter,* IV (1955), 32.
26. *Les Constitutions Européennes* (Paris, 1951), I, 14 ff.

habit they discouraged the evolution of conventions designed to adapt the regime to local needs and prevented the ultimate assimilation of democratic values to national life. If Professor Mirkine's diagnosis is correct, there is perhaps less reason to feel apprehensive today. Professors Arnold Zurcher and Karl Loewenstein have assured us that the new constitutions framed at the end of World War II reflect little optimism and contribute few new ideas.[27] Men cannot be forever constructing the foundations of society, and political institutions cannot operate successfully if they are to be remodelled continuously in accordance with the demands of abstract reason. On the other hand, the importance of tradition ought not to be invoked constantly as a defense of the *status quo;* for under these circumstances society can make no progress. Burke pointed out that there is a middle ground between "absolute destruction" and "unreformed existence" and declared that it is the task of statesmen to find the middle ground.

In destroying the old Christian unity and admitting all beliefs and systems of opinion, it was not realized that a time might come when insanity would claim as much right to exist as reason and that the absence of universally accepted norms would reduce, if it did not eliminate, the capacity for choice. Thus one of the symptoms of this crisis of authority is a regression of judgment, a loss in the capacity to distinguish knowledge from belief, and the disappearance of that critical faculty which makes it possible for man to discriminate between what he knows, believes, or would like to believe, and what he is forced to observe.

An illustration of the loss of this faculty for self-criticism can be seen by examining current discussions involving revolution and conservation. Ever since the end of the nineteenth century an increasingly favorable emphasis has been placed upon the term revolution and a correspondingly unfavorable impression created for ideas described as conservative or traditional. To some extent this reflects

27. *Constitutional Trends Since World War II* (New York, 1951), pp. 3–8, 191–224. This is not altogether true; for the West German Constitution provides for a unique relationship between the Chancellor and the Bundestag and the Italian Constitution provides for a Constitutional Court. Moreover, the French Constitution of 1946 defines relationships in considerable detail and provides for institutions unprecedented in French constitutional life. A number of amendments have recently been added to the French Constitution; and although they are also quite detailed, their net effect is to approach more closely the practice of the Third Republic.

the frustrations and legitimate feelings of discontent associated with the times; but it also manifests a negative attitude towards whatever exists. As a matter of fact, things have gone so far in France that no deputy or party can afford to tolerate being called conservative; and an outstanding French scholar has recently stated that

> Reading any of the French publications written during the last ten years by French intellectuals for their fellows, one cannot fail to notice that, for all of them, *subversion is ontologically superior to non-subversion, revolution ontologically superior to its opposite, or even to the mere absence of revolution.*[28]

Under these circumstances man finds himself on an ideological merry-go-round; for the communists are then free to admit those who serve their interests into the glory of revolutionary grandeur and denounce those who stand in the way as "reactionary" or "fascist." Thus political logic is sacrificed to purely emotional slogans, superficial analogies, and arbitrary generalizations. Moreover, such notions ignore the first principles of society. Man is by nature a conservative creature, and he must by necessity absorb much of his wisdom from society. The most disturbing thing, however, about this kind of attack upon conservation is not its stupidity but the extent to which it has been commonly considered normal and natural.

Such intellectual nihilism is a pathological condition; but it was generated by unwarranted generalizations based upon limited or false hypotheses.

> Because some of these norms have disappointed him, he [the intellectual] is convinced that others can hardly be worth more. And this frustration leads to an arbitrary egalitarianism to which all norms appear as equivalent and are thus reduced to the level of ideologies. The category of the quantitative is falsely applied to what is essentially qualitative—for, if there is some sense in stating that all men are equal, there obviously is no sense whatever in claiming that all ideas have the same merit.[29]

The West has the intellectual resources to free itself from this type of mechanical sophistry. It can turn to a more systematic study of politics and the nature of man; it can recognize that the false

28. Jules Monnerot, "Intellectual Nihilism and the Crisis of Authority," *Confluence,* III (1954), 437–438.
29. *Ibid.,* p. 439.

premises of liberalism produced an equally one-sided counter-philosophy in Marxism; and by recognizing the excessive material-ism and falsehoods in both, it will discover anew the Christian view of man and society. As political science has become more conscious of its limitations and as it has improved its methods in an attempt to acquire more knowledge, an increasing number of intellectuals have found inspiration in the Hebrew-Christian tradition.[30]

Although many people in Europe are still glaring at each other through the angry masks of obsolete ideologies and although dis-appointment in old illusions does not necessarily create a new ap-petite for political reality, still there is some reason to feel more hopeful today. Germany, Austria, Finland, and Belgium were the scenes of latent or civil war in the 1930's; but these countries now show a new capacity for attending harmoniously to the conduct of public affairs. In France political warfare appears to be less violent than it was in the past and political tension appears to be ebbing year by year. Even in countries which do not show this process of civic reconciliation there is some reason to feel that the intensity with which violent political illusions are held has de-creased. Thus "the shattering floods raised by the Russian Revolu-tion seem to be receding in Europe even while they are still mount-ing higher in Asia." [31] All of this augurs well for democracy and indicates that Europe may be entering a new stage of political de-velopment in which the prospects for a lasting establishment of free institutions will be greatly improved.

3. Pluralist nature of society. The entire life of man is not coterminous with the state; for in every society there must be lesser units of government and a host of voluntary associations in which the citizen can participate and pursue his own individual interests. Christianity emphasizes the distinction between the things that are Caesar's and the things that are God's; the Church has always held that the state is not an end in itself; and even after the secularization of politics when state absolutism was no longer resisted in the name of the Church, democratic thinkers argued that natural law con-

30. John H. Hallowell, *The Moral Foundations of Democracy* and *Main Currents in Modern Political Thought* (New York, 1950), pp. 618–695; Gurian and Fitzsimons, *op. cit.,* pp. 2–8; Ernest S. Griffith, "Cultural Prerequisites to a Suc-cessfully Functioning Democracy," *The American Political Science Review,* L (March, 1956), 101–115.

31. Polanyi, *op. cit.,* p. 33.

ferred upon the citizen individual rights. One of the weaknesses of modern liberal philosophy is its tendency to think in terms of the national state composed of atomistic individuals with nothing in between. Such a conception does not give sufficient opportunity for man to exercise his creative ability and ignores the fact that both power and loyalties must be dispersed. In this sense the democratic state is pluralistic, not monolithic or total; and although the state may be supreme in some spheres, it must not be all-inclusive and deprive the citizen from finding the deeper purposes of life.[32]

4. Realistic attitude towards property. Classic liberalism viewed the ownership of property as an inalienable right and sought to emancipate property relations from all political control by assigning to the legal owner practically an unlimited control over his possessions. Marxism, which arose as a reaction to the excesses of rugged individualism, ascribed the origin of all social evils to the private ownership of property and sought to establish social harmony by placing all productive property in the hands of the state. It has previously been pointed out that the social conflict engendered by these opposing views on property has threatened the whole democratic process and contributed towards the disintegration of representative institutions in a number of countries. Today every modern government plays an important role in economic affairs; and although there is considerable variation in the extent to which property is owned and operated by the state, both Marxists and extreme conservatives still confuse the issue by describing the existing economy in terms of free enterprise and free competition and by insisting that the choice is between an unbridled capitalism and a thorough-going socialism.

Democracy involves a faith in the future and a belief that man is capable of improvement, and much of the gloom and despair felt at the present time can be traced to a tacit acceptance of Marxist principles. Marx cast the future in an iron mold by proclaiming an inevitable law of history and a dialectical process to which mankind can only conform. He described legal and political institutions as merely the forceful instruments of class rule and denied the

32. John Courtney Murray, "The Problem of Pluralism in America," *Thought*, XXIX (June, 1954), 165–208 and "On the Structure of the Church-State Problem," in Gurian and Fitzsimons (eds.), *op. cit.*, pp. 11–32; Maritain, *Man and the State*, pp. 19–27; MacIver, *The Web of Government*, pp. 421–446.

existence of an objective state. At the time in which he wrote modern democracy was still in its infancy and it was possible, as indeed it still is, to cite many examples of class pressures upon government; but Marx failed to foresee the extent to which democracy has been developing through the years and foreclosed in his theory even the possibility that government can be anything other than the rule of a narrow class interest. Such a conception has many anti-democratic implications and is hostile to the presuppositions of democracy. As H. B. Mayo has said,

> So far as the Marxist philosophy of history is believed, even though it is false, to that extent it tends to weaken the will to democracy, encourages a fatalistic submission to communist movements, and postpones freedom of choice for mankind until the far future and the arrival of the classless society. Anyone who really believes in the inevitable victory of communism is lost as a democrat.[33]

If Marx's general theory is correct and if the economic foundation of society is all that matters, it may be argued that politics is of no real importance. Moreover, the Marxist is unable to explain the hostility of business in modern society toward its alleged puppet, the state. Non-revolutionary socialists, such as the Fabians and revisionist parties on the Continent, argue that a violent break with the past need not take place and that political institutions can be consciously and flexibly adapted to changing economic conditions. However, to the extent that some of these parties advocate extreme class consciousness, represent the narrow interests of only a single group, and view politics as merely the means for capturing the state in order to "smash" the system and establish a new order, they espouse a doctrine inconsistent with the genius of democracy.

Although the conflict of opposing ideas on property has now gone so far that knowledge alone will not eliminate the controversy, still the key to a solution can perhaps best be found by examining the nature of the economy and by analyzing contemporary economic trends without prejudice. Society is always undergoing peaceful adaptation and the economy has been developing continuously since the days of Adam Smith and Karl Marx. Fortunately a great deal of careful scholarship has been devoted to this subject in the United States. For example, it is generally agreed that a few large

33. Mayo, *op. cit.*, p. 290.

firms have increasingly come to dominate the productive industries, that small entrepreneurs exist in larger numbers than ever before particularly in the expanding services and distributive trades, and that small firms are doing a steadily declining proportion of the country's business in mining, power, finance, and some manufacturing industries. On the other hand, it is also generally agreed that large-scale enterprise has many advantages which the world cannot do without if it wants the mass consumption which only mass production can make possible. Berle and Means have called attention to the fact that the ownership of stock is more widely dispersed than is generally supposed, that in only a few of the two hundred largest corporations in the United States do a small number of stockholders own a majority of the stock, and that the most important change taking place in American capitalism is the divorce between ownership and control.[34] Since legal ownership is scattered among a host of small stockholders, actual control is falling more and more into the hands of a high-salaried executive class. In a subsequent and more important study Adolf Berle, Jr. has attempted to show the significance of these developments.[35] He says that as professional management has replaced the management of the private owner a more socialized concept of corporate responsibility has been brought to the direction of "big business." As a matter of fact, he thinks that the directors of a large corporation, who are freed from the importunate and immediate demands of stockholders, are far more interested in favorable public relations than in the size of the firm's profits and that they recognize a greater social responsibility than was possible in a society consisting of a large number of small business men. Moreover, Professor John K. Galbraith has called attention to the tendency of power to beget a countervailing or offsetting power and argues, at least by implication, that governmental intervention is unnecessary beyond what may be needed to encourage countervailing power among those at present weak and unorganized.[36]

Whatever weight may be assigned to these two interpretations

34. Adolf A. Berle, Jr. and Gardiner C. Means, *The Modern Corporation and Private Property* (New York, 1937) and *The Distribution of Ownership in the 200 Largest Non-financial Corporations* (Washington, D.C.: T.N.E.C. Monograph No. 29, 1941).

35. *The Twentieth Century Capitalist Revolution* (New York, 1954).

36. *The Concept of Countervailing Power* (Boston, 1952).

of the "new capitalism," there can be little doubt that American industry has shown an amazing capacity to increase and improve production and that American private corporations have developed a social role quite different from enterprise in most areas of the world. Thus American government has not had to deal with the dangerous, and perhaps impossible, administrative burden of nationalized industry, has avoided direct responsibility for improving the living standards of the people, and has fortunately escaped the difficulties experienced by European post-war democracies in compromising partisan differences growing out of broad issues involving state responsibility for economic and social welfare.

There is considerable reason to doubt whether the American experience can be transplanted to the Continent of Europe. This is partially because of the unique nature of American capitalism and also because European capitalism has never achieved a success comparable to that of the United States. On the Continent investors have been less inclined to take risks; they have concentrated upon a sure market rather than upon policies designed to expand production; and they have pursued short-sighted personnel policies which, together with a social system restricting opportunity, have fostered a deep-seated feeling of class bitterness absent in the United States. European capitalism, therefore, is commonly considered as a monopolistic, unimaginative, bureaucratic conspiracy for scarcity rather than plenty and as an economic system designed to withhold from the masses their rightful heritage and their human dignity. A knowledge of how widespread this feeling is explains why traditional capitalist notions are unacceptable and why both socialism and communism enjoy a large following. However, there is reason to believe that the modern capitalist revolution is having some effect. Barbara Ward has recently called attention to the fact that profound changes are taking place in European socialist thinking and that an increasing number of Europeans are now prepared "to look at the economic and social reality with a fresh and undogmatic eye." [37] For example, German trade unions have preferred output to wage inflation and participation in management to state control; but, as might be expected, it is in Britain, where the Labor party was never wedded to a dogmatic and uncompromising Marx-

37. See Barbara Ward, "A Fresh Look at the Profit Motive," *The New York Times Magazine* (April 29, 1956), pp. 12, 42–47.

ism and where actual experience with nationalized industries has compelled the abandonment of old slogans, that the ideological barriers are beginning to come down. However, it would be unrealistic to argue that this trend has gone very far outside of Britain; for although experience refutes the illusions in both liberal and Marxist theories of property, a realistic and dynamic doctrine has thus far failed to take their place.

The traditional Christian view of property would appear to supply a common denominator able to mitigate the class struggle and reduce it to proportions which would not threaten the whole democratic process; for the Church has always held that the nature of man requires the ownership of property but that his aggressive nature necessitates social control. However, an effective social philosophy must be more than an ingenious mixture of liberal and socialist principles; for it cannot have a decisive and permanent influence unless it is based on sound principles and has an identity of its own. Although socialism and communism have arisen as a reaction to injustices in the economic system, a Marxian solution would concentrate power at the center and thereby destroy human freedom. The liberal philosophers were right in seeing a vital connection between the ownership of property and personal freedom; but an argument of this kind supported by an appeal to natural law is of little concern to the man who owns no property. It follows that it is the duty of the state to multiply the number of property owners, to sponsor programs designed to disperse ownership, and to promote profit sharing and stock ownership among the workers.

To state general principles is easy; to implement them in practice is more difficult. Too often philosophers have been content to demonstrate the excellence of their principles without attempting to show how they could be applied in practice. It is not enough, therefore, to demonstrate the truth of one's principles and the falsity of those held by opponents; for history records many instances when a superior philosophy failed to gain adherents because its supporters were unsuccessful in demonstrating how it could be applied in practice. Although it is perhaps impossible to draw up a permanent program which contains a final solution and although actual policies will differ considerably from country to country in accordance with varying economic conditions, political parties can make practical suggestions only on the basis of greater knowledge of actual conditions. The average man, who does not know philosophy, can understand a program that is definite and specific; and policies based upon justice will have a wide appeal. From this point of view the greatest danger to democracy is timidity, the lack of imagination, and an unconscious doubt in the validity of Christian principles. There is no evidence to indicate that man is really as aggressive, self-centered, and uncooperative as politicians frequently suppose. As Reinhold Niebuhr has pointed out,

> A free society requires some confidence in the ability of men to reach tentative and tolerable adjustments between their competing interests and to arrive at some common notions of justice which transcend all partial interests. A consistent pessimism in regard to man's rational capacity for justice invariably leads to absolutistic political theories; for they prompt the conviction that only preponderant power can coerce the various vitalities of a community into a working harmony. . . . Man's capacity for justice makes democracy possible; but man's inclination to injustice makes democracy necessary.[38]

Conclusion

It is impossible to state with certainty the future of democracy in the modern world. Man as a free agent has the capacity to choose and the ability to influence his destiny. However, the social sciences lack certainty, and the present state of our knowledge can take us only a small way in determining the outcome.

Emphasis has been placed upon our lack of knowledge and the need for more study because existing theories do not seem to explain adequately political events and because profound changes taking place at the present time are little understood and their significance often ignored. However, there is a sense in which a solution to the crisis does not depend upon more knowledge. As Professor Hans J. Morgenthau has pointed out, "Politics is an art and not a science, and what is required for its mastery is not the rationality of the engineer but the wisdom and moral strength of the statesman." [39] The political conflicts in the modern world are only partially economic; they are not technical problems to be resolved through a blueprint; and they are similar to irrational forces that have previously dominated the aspirations of man. Man

38. Reinhold Niebuhr, *The Children of Light and the Children of Darkness,* pp. x–xi.
39. *Scientific Man vs. Power Politics* (Chicago, 1946), p. 10.

is a rational creature, but he is also influenced by prejudice and emotion; and it is impossible to predict with certainty whether the immediate future lies with the democratic leader or the tyrannical demagogue. The question confronting the modern world is whether it has the capacity to produce the statesmen who have the political wisdom to act successfully, who have the moral judgment to choose among expedient actions the least evil ones, and who have the imagination to build a new society which will reconcile man's political nature with his moral aspirations and his weakness with his strength.

Index

parliamentary government in, 35-36, 69-70, 93, 154-155
personal character of history, 113
unification in, 8, 54
See also Fascism.

Jefferson, Thomas, 2, 136
Jennings, W. Ivor, 57n
Jewkes, John, 140n

Kantorowicz, Hermann, 20n
Keckskemeti, Paul, 122-123
Kelsen, Hans, 27n, 77n
Kemal Pasha, Mustafa, 19, 22-23, 26, 111, 112
Kendall, Willmoore, 136n
Kingsley, John D., 100n
Kirchheimer, Otto, 147n
Kirdoff, Emil, 91
Kormos, C., 31n
Kraus, Herbert, 61n
Kravchenko, Victor, 100n

Laissez-faire
See Democracy and Liberalism.
Langsam, Walter S., 30n
Laski, Harold J., 42, 55n, 132, 147n
Lasswell, Harold D., 78n, 120n, 160n
Latin America, 71-72, 79
Latvia, 4
Le Bon, Gustav, 125n
Lecky, William E. H., 2
Lederer, Emil, 126-127
Legislature
See Parliament.
Lehmann, Fritz, 79
Leites, Nathan, 122-123
Lenin, V. I., 27, 111
Letwin, Shirley R., 111n
Levinson, D., 120n
Liberalism,
achievements of, 163
assumptions of, 50
atomistic conception of, 161
and democracy, 9-10, 14, 55, 57, 59
Marxism as a reaction to, 167
and property, 167, 171
weaknesses of, 160-161, 165-166, 167
See also Democracy.
Liberty, 9-10, 98
and security, 100
Lindbloom, Charles E., 144n
Lindsay, A. D., 106-107
Lippmann, Walter, 18n
Lithuania, 4
Locke, John, 9, 136

Loewenstein, Karl, 4, 19, 33n, 40, 41, 54n, 147n, 153n, 156, 164
Lowell, A. Lawrence, 3n, 66n

McCloskey, Herbert, 136n
MacDonald, Ramsay, 114, 146
Machiavelli, Niccolo, 7
McIlwain, C. H., 7
MacIver, Robert M., 17n, 20, 47, 71-72, 85n, 88n, 133, 134, 167n
McKenzie, Robert T., 66n
Madison, James, 161
Majority, rule of
See Democracy.
Mannheim, Karl, 107n, 140n
Manuel, F. E., 44n, 95n
Maritain, Jacques, 160n, 167n
Marxism,
anti-democratic implications of, 167-168
and class conflict, 84-85, 93-96
criticism of, 78, 139, 167-168, 171
and democracy, 47
interpretation of dictatorship, 75-76
intolerance and uncompromising intransigence of, 95-96
and mass state, 126-128
one-sided nature of, 166
oversimplification of class conflict, 94-95
as a reaction to liberalism, 167
See also Dictatorship.
Masses,
democracy and rule of, 72, 139-140
despair of, 90
state of, 125-128
Mayo, H. B., 160, 168
Means, Gardiner C., 169
Merriam, Charles E., 77n
Metaxas, John, 5, 22
Middle class,
and absolutist state, 8
apprehensions of, 77
fear of majority rule, 76-77
increase in numbers and prosperity of, 78
support of fascism, 75-78
support of liberal democracy, 9-10
Military dictatorship, 22-27
in Poland, 23-25
in Spain, 25-26
in Turkey, 22-23
Mill, James, 2, 9
Mill, John Stuart, 2, 9, 39, 57, 71
Mills, C. Wright, 109n
Milton, John, 9

Portugal, 4, 43, 105
Primo de Rivera, Miguel, 4, 22
Propaganda
  See Dictatorship, National Socialism.
Property,
  and countervailing power, 169
  democratic control of, 51
  divorce between ownership and control, 169
  and personal freedom, 171
  social responsibility of, 169-170, 171-172
  traditional Christian view of, 171-172
Proportional representation, 37-38, 42n
  effect on political parties, 47, 61-65, 66
  and executive stability, 62-65
  F. A. Hermens on, 61-65
  in Weimar Germany, 47, 61, 66

Rappard, William E., 100n, 134-135
Raushenbush, Stephen, 31n
Revolution vs. conservation, 49-50, 76-77, 164-166
Rich, S. Grover, Jr., 25n, 26n
Roberts, Henry L., 22n
Robson, William A., 101n
Rogers, Lindsay, 19n, 38, 147n
Roosevelt, Franklin D., 112
Röpke, Wilhelm, 96
Rossi, Ernesto, 144n
Rossiter, Clinton L., 38n, 147n
Roucek, Joseph S., 22n
Royal dictatorship, 21-22
  in Bulgaria, 21
  in Greece, 22
  in Rumania, 22
  in Spain, 22
  in Yugoslavia, 21
Rumania, 4, 19, 22, 31
Russia,
  Bolshevik revolution, 3, 27, 78
  bureaucracy in, 100
  collapse of Tsarist regime, 2
  economic planning in, 141
  hero-worship in, 111
  party dictatorship in, 27, 30, 84
  social classes in, 29, 133-134

Salvemini, Gaetano, 36
Sanford, Nevitt, 120n
Saposs, David J., 78n
Schneider, Herbert W., 36n, 111n
Schuman, Frederick L., 92n, 120n, 128
Schumpeter, Joseph A., 141n

Schwartz, Harry, 100n
Schwartz, Solomon M., 134n
Scott, Jonathan F., 22n
Sforza, Carlo, 19n
Simon, Yves, 135n, 140n, 161n
Smith, Adam, 9
Social Democrats (Germany),
  social composition of membership, 80
Social stratification
  See Dictatorship, Fascism, Marxism, National Socialism.
Soviet Union
  See Russia.
Spain, 4-5, 8, 22, 25-26, 43-44, 47, 70, 95
Spearman, Diana, 19n, 20n, 23, 33n, 93n, 96n, 118n, 129
Speier, Hans, 87n, 133
Spencer, Henry R., 19n, 36n
Stalin, Josef, 27-28, 111
Stamps, Norman L., 34n
Starr, Joseph R., 4n
State,
  absolutist period characterized, 9
  of amorphous masses, 125-128
  derivation of term, 7-8
  effect of evolution on political institutions, 12-15
  emphasis on welfare, 10-11, 102
  evolution of, 8-15, 53-55
  rise of nation state, 7-9
  See also Democracy, Liberalism.
Steiner, H. Arthur, 151n
Strachey, John, 76n
Sulzberger, C. L., 157n
Switzerland, 1, 63, 147

Thomson, C. A., 44n
Thyssen, Fritz, 91, 92n
Tingsten, Herbert, 82n, 83n
Turkey, 4, 22-23, 26, 93, 111, 159
Tyranny
  See Dictatorship.

Vignaux, Paul, 105n

Ward, Barbara, 170
Watkins, Frederick M., 38n
Webb, Beatrice, 111
Webb, Sidney, 104n, 111
Weber, Max, 109
Weimar Constitution
  See Germany.
Weiner, Myron, 48n